DEER & THUNDER

DEER & THUNDER

INDIGENOUS WAYS OF
RESTORING THE WORLD

BY ARKAN LUSHWALA

ISBN-13: 978-1976511677
ISBN-10: 1976511674
Arkan Lushwala, Ribera, New Mexico

EDITED BY TIMOTHY P. MCLAUGHLIN
BOOK DESIGN BY SOPHIE COOPER

Dedicated to the memory of Jeannie Kerrigan,
Bill Brave Heart & Martin Paucar.

CONTENTS

PART TWO: THUNDER

FOREWORD

This is a wondrous and mysterious moment in human history, a critical time in which we have the opportunity to restructure our relationship to the natural world and hopefully help engender its great healing. This restructuring is certainly long overdue. As we open our eyes to the lasting harmful impacts of our industrialized, and now technologized, society upon the total ecology, it becomes evident we have neglected the need to reciprocate the Earth for the many gifts we constantly harvest from her body. How can we, a species that harmoniously drew from and replenished our living environments for countless centuries, have severely depleted the Earth's resources in such a short span and recklessly left ourselves and all other forms of earthly life in very real peril? More importantly, how can we restore that harmonious, reciprocal dynamic with the beautiful system of life on this planet?

In navigating our way through these paramount

concerns, more and more of us have arrived at the same guidepost that excitingly announces: Something about what ancient people knew and practiced must be highly relevant for us today. For we have come to a perplexing and fascinating stage in our development as humans, a paradoxical state of supreme advancement coupled with diminutive understanding. We know how to do nearly anything but have largely lost or belittled the foundational wisdom about what to do or why to do it. Our minds are keen but in some sense they have become misguided and leave us bewildered and bereft. And so, thankfully, humanity is circling back toward an appreciation, even a growing reverence, of indigenous wisdom, seeking the original why of things so we will again know what actions to take.

In response to this necessary awakening, my spiritual brother and mentor, Arkan Lushwala, has laid out, in a delightful mix of stark clarity and playful levity, the principles by which his Andean ancestors lived and flourished upon the Earth. Principles so simple they fill the mind, and the heart, with great peace. And principles so profound the many nuances of their truths are absorbed over a lifetime. Or, more accurately, over a lineage of many generations, like that of the Andean people, who keep renewing the essence of these principles and continually discern how to abide by them. Lacking a universal human culture, we can only each work at piecing together the threads of a new way, discovering step-by-step how to apply ancient wisdom to complex modern realities.

The journey begins by sinking into the indigenous mind that speaks to us in the pages of this book, by trying on a perspective of observance more than analysis, of allowance rather than control. Arkan shows us how the old ones prioritized aligning and flowing with the energies of Nature — honoring them as powerful forces activated through intimate relationship — where the contemporary person has become habituated with impersonally harnessing the Earth's energies as disposable commodities. The more we feel into the shape of the ancient human heart, the more we realize no well-structured law or policy will bring about the shift needed in the modern human heart. Only by collectively falling back in love with the Earth again and again will we once more understand how to be her adoring, and very useful, sons and daughters.

I vividly remember the first time I met Arkan. I had just moved to New Mexico after serving for several years as an educator on the Pine Ridge Reservation in South Dakota and my being was still vibrating from deep immersion into all the beauty and complexity of an indigenous community. Eager to sustain that vibration, I had gladly accepted an invitation from my spiritual grandfather, Basil Brave Heart, to a Lakota Sun Dance ceremony he was hosting in the New Mexican desert. As I sat at the drum, just beginning the second day of simmering in that thick stew of voice and rhythm and movement, a new dancer floated into the central circle. He moved differently from the others, his body nearly leaping through the steps with vigor. And his spirit had a brightness to it that was unmistakable. Yes, there was some South American flare aglow there, but there was also a quality all its own, something both commanding and vulnerable that spoke directly to me. Whatever that brightness was, it seized my attention and I felt certain I was meant to know and work with this man in some way. And so it has been. For over fifteen years, I have prayed in community with Arkan, through many ceremonies, both Lakota and Andean, and over many seasons. And now we step together in brotherhood at the Sun Dance, making of ourselves an offering to our beloved Earth and to the mystical Star Nations.

Most of all, I have been fed by his teachings, so often delivered orally in the humble setting of a willow lodge built close to the Earth's body. And I am beyond elated these vital teachings will be shared among more circles of humans whose souls are hungry for truths they can sense but may have yet to hear articulated in this special and intimate way. It has been a distinct privilege to work as the editor of this book. As much as possible, I have aspired to help the text stay true to Arkan's signature style as an oral teacher and the way he powerfully spins intersecting webs of magic through his insights, his stories, and the guidance gifted to him in ceremony. Throughout our collaboration, Arkan's spirit shined brightly with inspiration, though it must be a formidable challenge to write in English, the second language from the mother tongue in which he richly formed much of his indigenous perspective. In my estimation, Arkan has brilliantly wielded this adopted language to communicate something humanity is longing to hear and follow.

Deer and Thunder is a treasure for the impoverished human mind, a feast for the hungry human soul, and a balm for the aching human heart. Read it quietly and allow its instructions, alternately gentle and firm, to wash through you. And speak it aloud, bringing others into its wondrous enchantment and its wise insistence. If a text, by virtue of the prayer and medicine woven into its making, can become a ceremony, then *Deer and Thunder* is just that: an ongoing, renewable, living ceremony.

- Timothy P. McLaughlin, 2017

INTRODUCTION

Throughout my life, it has been an honor to watch my elders make medicine in their mouths and feed the world with their tender sacred speech. Following their example, I want to share words that make waterfalls, lakes and rivers, and offer some medicine to those who are wondering how we will continue living when the Earth that sustains our lives is so damaged. What I share here, far from being my own creation, is ancient memory that belongs to all of us.

One of my dear Elders was a Q'ero man from up in the mountains of the Cusco area named Martin Paucar. Several years ago at a Lakota Sun Dance held in New Mexico, Tayta Martin had come from Peru to participate in the ceremony. To perform the ceremony, we needed four consecutive sunny days and the forecast instead predicted four days of intense rains, so my Tayta Martin accepted the awesome responsibility of moving the clouds for us to be able to dance! He spent every day of the ceremony blowing his *pututo*, a sort of Andean trumpet made of a conch shell, while keeping his gaze fixed on the sky and praying to the *Apukuna*, the spirits of the mountains, for the rain to go to another place where it may be more needed during those days. Thanks to his powerful prayer, we had four days of sunshine!

At the end of the ceremony, we were all tired and happily feasting together when Tayta Martin said to us: "That was really hard. So many times it almost rained. I was praying to my mountains in Peru but the clouds kept coming. I realized I had to make friends with the mountains here. I had to explain to them that I am a *Pampamisayuq* and the people were counting on me. With tender words, I asked them to consider what the people would say if it rained after all I had done. I begged them not to make me look bad!" His levity made us laugh so hard and we were all very grateful to him as well as amazed at his deeply intimate relation to the spirits of Nature.

After the ceremony, he prepared an offering to thank the mountains, the thunders and all of Pachamama for having heard our prayers. Tayta Martin was happy and kept telling us stories about different occasions when he was asked to call the rain or to make it stop. Once, in Peru, he was even hired by a mining company whose activities depended on the abundance of a lake high in the mountains that was becoming dry.

The engineers of the company decided he was the only one that could resolve the problem. And he did. After he made the offerings to the mountains surrounding the lake, it began to rain, and so much rain fell that the lake became full again!

In speaking about the gifts of my elder, I do not want to impress anyone. My intention is to share the spiritual depths of a culture that creates individuals like my *tayta,* ones with a real capacity to have an influence on the health of the Earth. I am one of those who believe all of humanity can regain an ancient way of being that allows us to talk to our Mother Earth to resolve dangerous imbalances of the environment under her guidance. The state of humans and the state of the Earth are completely intertwined, and the full recovery of the best of our human nature will be the healing of Nature.

At this time, living under the threat of global warming and climate change, it is very useful to observe the original peoples of the Earth and recall practices humans developed over thousands of years to adapt to the various changes of Nature. In the thick of the current environmental crisis, it is useful to know there are still people who have the power to call rain or to move the clouds when there is too much rain. The people of our Andean indigenous communities, largely labeled as people without education, inherently understand how our dances have the power to make rain and why the offerings we ceremonial leaders prepare can help to heal damaged lands. This knowledge that we dance with, alive and joyful, is our inheritance; it is a collective way of being that will help us continue living on Earth. It is the memory of the ancient Earth People.

There were tribes of Earth People in Europe too, long ago, white-skinned indigenous people who were forced to change their ways in the same way they have been trying to change ours for centuries. The campaign to eradicate indigenous peoples did not begin in what is now called the Americas but in Europe long before the Spaniards arrived on this continent. For centuries, kings and then popes subjugated ancient European tribes until there wasn't one person left who could openly practice any spirituality based primarily on loving the Earth.

When they arrived on our continent, the European authorities simply continued the practices they had used in their lands to suppress the natural tendencies of their own people. They worked diligently to create a society of Christians and erase the societies of tribal people; but here they didn't succeed as well as they had in Europe. In many places of the Andes and the Amazon, the relationship between ancient communities and the heart of their lands is very strong to this day. However, there are still strategies in place aimed to make us abandon our Earth-based ways of life and our precious lands. Some of those strategies, executed over more than five hundred years, are becoming more successful in this modern world as indigenous youth now tend to leave their rural homelands looking for work or modernity and end up turning their back on the traditions of their grandparents.

Once people's hands are taken away from the Earth, they are well on their way to forgetting she is their mother. It may take a couple generations, but it eventually happens. Indigenous people uprooted from their community and land could in time become like schizophrenics as they hear different voices simultaneously wanting very different things. Some are voices of the modern world offering them progress, comfort and power. The others, impossible to silence, are the voices of our ancestors vibrating in their blood, telling them to go back to the Earth, to remember their heart.

When this split of the human soul happened to European indigenous people long ago, there were no corporations wielding influence. Instead there were powerful families whose enterprises required the common people to serve their interests and surrender their own power and connection to the Earth. People of European descent who know their history might be able to identify how and when their ancestors were separated from the wisdom of the Earth and lost access to the direct guidance of the infinite intelligence that circulates in the Universe.

What we all know intimately, Indigenous and Europeans alike, is that at some point, amongst other things, it became shameful to eat with our hands and have our feet naked and dirty. Indigenous parents aspiring to assimilate their children into the modern world and its "better opportunities" punish them when they eat with their hands or when their feet are soiled because they love them and want them to be respected by the rest of the world. In old Europe, the common people also emulated the ways of the nobles in the kings' courts so they wouldn't be seen as savages and dismissed from social circles that offered opportunities for a better life. The truth is that on the deepest level, there isn't much difference between what has happened to us in the Americas during the last centuries and what happened to the common peoples of Europe during the dark ages of medieval times.

The secret hope of the poor is that if you look and act like someone of a higher social class, you may end up becoming one. And even if you do not reach a higher level of society, perhaps your children will. In the Andes, the beautiful, natural and very healthy houses made with mud blocks are considered the houses of the poor, while the houses made out of bricks, cement, and iron that are infused with loads of chemical products are considered houses of "noble" material. Once a family has abandoned their indigenous community and accumulated some wealth, they build a house of "noble" material and believe they have acquired a higher social status.

It is understandable that parents who love their children would prefer they become part of a higher social class, people seen as having a better life with bigger houses and more food at the table and with more power in the world. Also people are seen as superior when they are educated, more intellectually developed and not considered ignorant. In addition to eating with fork and knife and wearing proper clothing and shoes, becoming an intellectual has become a new way to adopt the life of a higher class. Some indigenous people believe they will be more respected if they speak as if they are highly educated as well as if they look like they possess material wealth. Imagine those who are fluent in a native language and highly educated in indigenous culture but don't speak the language of the dominant society well. They will be subject to lots of criticism and teasing from others. In order to avoid this shame, they will do everything possible not to look or sound like indigenous people and therefore many of the Native traditions and languages are dying.

People of European descent, as human as we Andean people are, also prefer to avoid shame. In classist societies, a large number of modern people of all backgrounds use their limited time and energy diligently trying not to look like Indians or "savages" in the hope of being rather superior and gaining the respect of a higher social class. Following costly trends and fashion, they make immense efforts to acquire goods that show their social status, and have no energy left to speak to their Mother, the Earth, to remember the pace of her rhythm, to feel the blessing of a night spent asleep on her body, to receive the medicine of drinking directly from her springs. They are always at risk of becoming too comfortable and separate from the Earth, which makes their body more inclined to illnesses. Just a little research can uncover scientific studies whose results demonstrate that eating with one's hands and having one's naked feet touch the ground regularly makes humans healthier and more energized. The sterilized human whose feet are insulated from the land by always wearing shoes and who never touches the food they eat requires high doses of caffeine or sugar to feel energized. Of course it is understandable that most people prefer to avoid being teased or disrespected for acting in ways that make them look like outdated Earth People; but now we have to consider that our Mother Earth is also paying a high price for the over-consumption of modern societies.

I see the good intentions of those who believe in modernity and are truly convinced that economic development in our rural areas will bring our people out of poverty and reduce their suffering. But it is important to recognize there are different kinds of poverty. Lack of intimate contact with the sacredness of Nature and the lack of warmth and support from a community are sources of enormous suffering for most modern people. Actually, this type of poverty and hunger leads teenagers to look for drugs regardless of how wealthy their families are. The children of the rich and the poor buy drugs in the same places. The impoverished souls of the youngsters look for nourishment in the wrong places, becoming chronically intoxicated as they try to free their mind from the grasp of a toxic world. As a result, they end up causing much suffering to themselves and their families.

The loss of the memory of an indigenous humanity has allowed the growth of a distracted and destructive way of life. The damage inflicted upon humanity and our Mother Earth has gone so far that thankfully many people are now waking up, are remembering again, and more and more individuals and groups are seeking to remember the natural ways of the original Earth People and their sacred way of life. Together with other forms of social transformation, the green revolution is arriving, a revolution that for people determined to develop humanly and spiritually isn't just about using different technologies to generate clean energy. It has a great deal to do with becoming human beings with a clean energy of our own, closer to our original nature.

As we work to build a healthy world, we cannot just

incorporate new technologies into the same culture that created the old ones. We need to create a new cultural context, one centered more in the heart, to give a real foundation for changing to cleaner forms of energy that do less harm to our lands and water sources. Creating this new culture can be more about remembering than inventing. In our genes, all human beings carry the memory of the ancient Earth People who moved with the rhythm of the Stars and the Earth, who were one with their lands, one with each other in communitarian life, and able to follow the guidance of Nature to make it through extremely difficult times, such as the Ice Age.

In some ways, the work is already happening. There are so many people longing to remember the original wisdom of humanity that a movement of a re-indigenization has begun. For now, it is occurring on a small scale as groups of people worldwide learn Earth-based forms of spiritual development by traveling to the places where we indigenous people hold our traditions and do our ceremonies. There are also many of us who are carriers of those ancient traditions and travel around the world when invited to share these ways of prayer and communication with the natural sources of life and health. Will this movement grow so that scores and scores of people all over the planet will develop the power to influence the health of the lands and waters that sustain our lives, like my dear Tayta Martin used to do?

The growth of this movement to re-indigenize humanity inspired me to write this book. I am aware that many of those men and women of European descent and mixed heritages who seek to recover the wisdom of their indigenous ancestors wish to deepen their work beyond just putting on some feathers, learning a few tribal songs or becoming dependent on the consumption of visionary plant medicines. My wish is to share the pillars of our ancient cultures so that people can engage with this work from that deeper place they are longing to find within themselves.

Some good-hearted individuals who take action in favor of the movement toward the re-emergence of Earth People are still conditioned by the individualistic and competitive drive of modern life, motivated by their personal needs, and so the much larger motivating forces haven't truly landed in them yet. For now, they continue to seek personal success when participating in indigenous activities, even when indigenous people have always first considered the well-being of the group. We are not very good at winning individual awards. The stage is too small for an indigenous person to receive an award because we would bring all those who participated in winning it onstage with us: family and community members, as well as deer, jaguars and dolphins, the thunders, the lakes and our huge mountains! In indigenous cultures, our actions are communitarian and our communities are composed of humans as well as the powers of nature and the sacred spirits. The making of something real always involves the participation of a whole community of life.

My friend, Manari Ushigua from the Sapara tribe in Ecuador, once said something really beautiful to a group of people in California: "To be an indigenous person doesn't make someone important. To be a white person doesn't make someone important either. When you really see the truth of things, you realize life is a net where all forms of life are connected. This net is the only thing that is important. Indigenous people always feel and express gratitude for being part of this net of life. So if you live grateful, you are indigenous."

In the old days, when everyone was indigenous and we were not afraid of being small or being nothing, there was no need to remind someone of what my friend Manari so clearly said. But things have changed with the prevalent forgetfulness of modern society. Because of what they haven't remembered yet, people of the modern world who now participate in the traditions of indigenous cultures are sometimes accused of falling into a position of cultural appropriation. This provokes the question: When is it permissible to utilize aspects of indigenous culture offered to others by the indigenous people and when does it become an act of appropriation?

My adoptive father, Basil Brave Heart, an Oglala Lakota Elder from the Pine Ridge Reservation in South Dakota, once gave a really good answer to this question. He reminded us of the response of Chief American Horse in the late eighteen-hundreds to the same question: "People from other places can do our ceremonies as long as they do it like the Lakota do it."

After reflecting at length about this simple answer, I believe American Horse was not just speaking about respecting and following the traditional forms of the ceremonies. "The way the Lakota do it," as I have come to know well, is also with deep humility and with beautiful simplicity, guided by spirit, devoid of the need for personal recognition, and with lots and lots of humor! The Lakota, like many indigenous groups, know how to make a wonderful container for a magical encounter between humans and the sacred powers, a place where we can break free for a moment from the load of our human burdens and ask for the help we need to continue living. We share our ways because we know that we are all brothers and sisters, and that everyone needs help. We feel grateful when people come to receive help from our indigenous ways and welcome them with an open heart; and we ask that they take the time to learn well and not take short cuts or trivialize our ancient traditions as nothing more than a new trend.

PART ONE:
DEER

Deer Nation comes from the East.

Like the sunrise that makes the world clear again,

their teachings are gently offered to the people

with tender patience.

Clear instructions are the medicine of Deer.

CHAPTER ONE

AMARU

THE SACRED SERPENT

The ancient people of the Andes observed Nature at the deepest level in order to follow its guidance and become aware of that which has the most impact on the quality of human life. One of their most valuable accomplishments was the observation they made of a river of vital energy that constantly flows on Earth, and that is fed by the energy of human beings.

Humans are constantly generating energy that is released onto the surface of the Earth. This energy gathers and builds in a continuously flowing motion, then descends into the depths of the Earth and later ascends again to the surface to collect more energy. Because of its resemblance to the movements of a snake, our Andean ancestors called this circulation of energy

Amaru — the sacred serpent. This infinite circular movement, from the tops of the mountains above the land to the underbellies of the rocks in the depths of Mother Earth, produces and increases the plasma of our planet. Plasma is pure vital energy of the highest frequency that is generated at inconceivably high temperatures in the Earth's core. It is a substance so rare and precious that it is capable of giving birth to new forms of energy and matter, and therefore necessary for the ongoing development of life on Earth.

In times when we need to realign ourselves with Nature in order to continue living, it is useful to remember our purpose. From this essential wisdom, we may find our way toward a promising future that is awaiting us. That very important and little known purpose of human life is to constantly deliver energy that feeds the formation of plasma in the Earth's core. And a crucial aspect of human life is that when feeding the Earth's plasma we can do it in two very different ways. We can do it unconsciously — through the energy we release in our daily activities, in our heavy emotions, incessant thoughts, endless conflicts, painful dramas and all kinds of natural expressions — or consciously by the deliberate production of high-frequency vibrations through artistic creations, prayer, celebration, sacred ceremonies and acts of deep compassion.

Our Andean culture was built upon this ancient knowledge. Some of the common occasions for making ceremonies to hand offerings with tenderness to the Earth are when some sort of illness affects a person, a family, or an entire community. The offerings purposely feed vitality into the Earth so the people don't have to feed her through their suffering. This energy consciously gifted to the Earth eventually circles back to us, carried by the power of Amaru, the sacred serpent, and brings healing to those that were sick and lost their vitality.

The ancient practice of making offerings is traditional to many peoples of the Earth and is an intentional, refined participation in the generation of energy that feeds the Earth's plasma. This practice can be as simple as praying to give thanks for the food we are about to eat, or developed through more complex ceremonies. Ceremonial leaders and healers identify "mouths" on the Earth where they place the highly charged offerings they prepare in order to feed her. In Runasimi, our indigenous language of the Andes commonly known as Quechua, we use the word *Ayni* to refer to these acts of reciprocity. *Ayni* is the principle of feeding all that feeds us, and we understand this action as the most basic and essential fulfillment of our purpose as humans. And because the movement of energy is circular, as we give vitality to the Earth, we receive vitality from the Earth. Those spiritual workers who place the offerings are also able to find places where the Earth releases enormous amounts of energy for the nourishment of our vitality, power spots on the land identified by our ancestors as the ideal settings for our spiritual practices and for growing food.

Nobody takes more life from the Earth than us humans, so it is our duty to give more nourishment to the Earth than any other species. It is our human responsibility to always feed the Earth that feeds us. When we forget how to consciously feed her from our heart's will, we eventually pay a much higher price, feeding her with our suffering and blood. Death and bloodshed liberate great amounts of energy. So, as cruel as it may seem, violent conflicts and wars have always contributed to the energy that the Earth uses to make plasma. Without consciously realizing it, the warriors of all nations in history served this purpose.

Throughout history, there have also been the wise and peaceful guides of humanity, individuals who were spiritually awake and proposed the healthiest ways of life. They were aware that the traumas of war produce cycles of destruction in which entire nations can stay trapped for a long time. Wars produce effects like illness, fear, shame and anger that can last many generations and perpetuate a human habit of feeding the Earth through suffering.

Over time, the effects of war have been extremely

harmful to us and, in the long run, to the Earth as well. The rise of societies with a closed heart, driven by self-defense, selfishness and greed, caused a chronic condition in which humans feed the Earth with their pains at the same time that they destroy her. In societies that forget to be grateful to the Earth, the energy released by human activities, in many cases destructive for the environment, is manipulated so it returns only to benefit some humans and is not freely gifted for the well-being of all life. This provokes the rise of an even greater hunger in a damaged Nature, an insatiable hunger that wants to take more energy from us. Some of the wealthiest nations in the world are often engaged in war, paying for their wealth and safety with the lives of their soldiers as well as the soldiers and innocent people of adversary nations.

Those enlightened guides of humanity have always voiced the peaceful alternative, that our societies develop and strengthen the cultural practices that produce high frequency energies to feed the Earth: ritual offerings, art, prayer, ceremony, humor, celebration, compassionate action and every manner of spiritual generosity. Even our economic activities can be infused with the healthy power of these practices and our gratitude to the Earth. Also, these practices help us discover the beauty of what we really are and develop our highest potential as human beings.

In peaceful societies the value of gold and silver is more spiritual than monetary; in violent societies spiritually damaged by incessant war, gold and silver are the desire of an insatiable hunger that simply creates more and more war. The conquest of our indigenous nations in the Andes was an encounter between two cultures that viewed gold and silver in very different ways. Finding gold was a principle motivation behind the enormous efforts of the invaders of our Andean world; paradoxically, they didn't know the real value of the sacred metal.

Ancient indigenous peoples who purposefully fed the energy in motion that the Earth uses to make plasma, extracted gold and silver as a sacred harvest, the tangible materializations of the powerful energy they had helped cultivate deep within the Earth. Those who adorned themselves with these metals for sacred ceremonies knew they were employing the fruits of their efforts and the gratitude of Mother Earth in the form of jewelry as devices to increase their capacity to listen to the Sun and be guided by information carried in the light that these metals powerfully absorb and reflect. In this way, they constantly increased their wisdom and their capacity to serve life.

One way or another, humans feed the Earth that feeds us. One undesirable way is through our suffering, whether in warfare or in the unconscious release of the roughest emotional, mental, physical and sexual energy. The other way is through the offering of well-prepared, refined human energies of the highest vibration. All human cultures and societies have done both. In today's world, once more we have a choice to make. In order to stop the accelerated destruction of Nature and the cycles of our own suffering, we need peace. From the perspective of ancient sages who lived in something of an earthly paradise and who left us temples so we could remember their wisdom, peace is not made by signed agreements between nations; it is an energy that has to be built and continually well fed. Peace is not the absence of war. Rather it is a conscious way of living wherein we choose to feed everything that feeds us so bloodshed is not needed as payment for all that we take from Nature.

My Q'ero elder Martin Paucar taught me to call this action of feeding the sources of our life *Haywarikuy*, meaning "to hand something to someone with tenderness." In the Andes, as in all ancient indigenous nations of the world, it is not out of obligation that we make offerings that bring life and prevent violence and suffering. We feel naturally drawn to hand the nourishment of our prayers into Pachamama's mouth, and we do so tenderly, our hearts filled with joy and overflowing with gratitude for all that our Mother gives us. Despite the hardships we sometimes have to endure living on this Earth and aware that we are always at risk of simply being food for her, we remain grateful because of the constant and generous opportunities we are all given to develop and become, instead, a brilliant guiding force serving all life. We can be food or we can be feeders, and this is a choice we have to make every day, many times a day.

CHAPTER TWO

ÑAWPARUNAKUNA

ANCESTORS

The Earth is so damaged by human activities that many people say it would be better if she got rid of us and saved herself together with all her other precious creatures. But saying this is another manifestation of the same forgetfulness that made us damage her. Humans are an essential part of the body of the Earth, and the Earth needs all her body parts in order to be whole and function well. After billions of years our planet reached a point in its development where the presence of humans was necessary. If that weren't true, we wouldn't be here. From their earliest emergence, indigenous communities from around the world have been aware of having a talent to serve the balance of life on Earth, just like bees, whales and trees. Therefore, in many different languages, we have called ourselves Earth People.

Through the spontaneous expression of their inherent talents, our ancestors realized they could serve as a guiding force working between the natural forces of order and chaos. As human beings, we have the capacity to generate vibrational frequencies that influence the balance of Nature and can even support the continuity of life itself. This is precisely what many original peoples of the Earth do today through rituals and sacred ceremonies: combine powerful energies and frequencies with the intention of nourishing the growth of all life. In this way, we are meant to be like musicians whose expressions have the power to bring life back into beauty and expansiveness. In fact, we are naturally highly skilled in the art of elevating the frequency of our reality to a level where illness and unhappiness disappear. Our ability to do this work comes from a humble listening to instructions issuing from the sacred sources of life. When we allow ourselves to be guided, we are capable of guiding.

Our ancestors, the *Ñawparunakuna* or ancient people, knew about the need to create places where they could receive sacred guidance. These were navels, places on the land where they grew an energetic umbilical cord that connected us to the Universal Mother who guides the development of all life. In ancient times, maintaining this umbilical connection to the Universal Intelligence was as essential to human societies as satellites and wireless communications are today.

The word *Cusco (Qosqo)* — the name of the city that was the center of the Inca world — means navel in our Runasimi language. *Taypi Kala* is the name in the Aymaran language for an even more ancient center that existed in the area of Lake Titiqaqa thousands of years before Cusco, and it also means navel. The most ancient and important temple in the central Andes is called *Chavin*, a name that comes from the word *Chawpin* that means "of the middle." When a person stands with legs planted on the Earth and arms extended toward the sky, the navel sits at the very middle of the body. Through prayer, deep observation, and familiarity with sacred geography, our ancestors were able to identify power spots on the Earth, pivotal points where a navel could be developed, and then built temples in and around those places. Tribes from many surrounding territories recognized these locations as the center of their world and referred to them as *Pakarina*, the place where life is born. When people of the old times wanted healing or instructions, they visited the navel temples. They trusted that what they received in those sacred places was rooted in a clean connection with the powers emanating from the Universal Mother rather than in mere human power. Ancient peoples would visit and revisit the navel places as often as necessary in order to remember themselves as children of the Earth and of the Universe. In these sacred sites, they reactivated their inborn sacred talents and continued their growth as skilled participants in the work of the Earth.

When people could not travel to the center of their world, the center extended itself towards them. Sacred energies emanated from the temples and radiated toward all the communities of very large territories. These invisible paths of energy were called *Seq'es* and they were constantly used. Ancient temples were not places of worship so much as powerful instruments. After being charged with cosmic power, they acted as distribution centers from where healing energy and sacred nourishment spread through the *Seq'es* in all directions. The food and seeds grown in the gardens and terraces of the temples where there was an umbilical connection with the Universe were charged with tremendous vitality and intelligence. Our ancestors made sure that these seeds could be sown and adapted in territories nearby and far away from the temple's location.

Considering the magnitude of all this, you can imagine what the loss of the temples meant for our ancestors during the conquest. At all costs, the guardians of the temples and their treasures had to find some way to keep the heart of their world alive and beating even when it became homeless. I have been told that when the ancient Hebrew people lost their temple for the second time and had to leave their homeland near

Jerusalem — the navel of their world — they transmitted the knowledge and memory of their sacred way of life into books. Using an alphabet in which the letters relate to a numerical system that gave enormous potency to the word-numbers, the Hebrew priests were able to construct a movable sacred home for their people, a home that could be built at any time and in any place simply by speaking it into existence. Indigenous people in the Andes didn't write books as the Hebrews did, so when we lost our temples of stone and clay, we learned to reproduce them on a very small scale, placing the main elements that gave them power into a small piece of fabric or paper. Where the Hebrews used words to build an invisible temple, we used, and still use, elements of the Earth such as flower petals, cotton balls, coca leaves, corn, seeds, shells, lama fat, little fruits, honey and other delicious nutrients.

The altar that we design over a small piece of paper with these elements is very simple, and amazingly it has the same quality and power as the ancient stone altars of the temples. It has a center, a navel, usually a shell, that connects the human-earthly world with the Cosmic Mother, and it has the right combination of colorful and delicious elements, carefully chosen and weighted like the Hebrew words. In the Andes, we are used to frequently building these altars that then become offerings charged with enormous vitality, made to provoke the birth of something missing, some energy that is needed for a healing to occur or for a hunger to subside and for balance to return.

Our offerings are burnt in a sacred fire. The tiny temples made of food, flowers and coca leaves then become smoke subtle enough to penetrate the essence of their destination and leave what is heavy in the ashes. In a similar way, Tibetan Lamas construct temples out of colored sand, then sweep them up and pour them into the flow of a stream. By letting them go with total detachment, what was communicated by the design of the offering-whether it be a request, an expression of gratitude, the intention of uniting opposite forces in order to generate new life or an alliance between humans and sacred powers-becomes part of the river of Universal Life. These offerings leave an imprint in the fabric of life, and this is how human beings influence the healthy development of all that lives on the Earth.

My life's honor is to be among those who today make umbilical connections with the universal sources of vitality and enact these powerful ceremonies. Those of us whose main job is to feed the Sacred are truly working with the Earth, in communication with her, and as part of her. Through our ritual offerings we feed the continuity of that which already is, acting like the mind of the Earth, nourishing and balancing all life within her great body. It is such an uplifting feeling to do something similar to what our ancestors did in the temples, somehow participating in the making of more life and guiding the same Universal Flow that guides us. We learn, from watching our elders, to maintain the keen attention of skillful dancers holding their sacred partner. The ancient indigenous spiritual workers of all nations whose practices we have kept alive were engaged in a permanent dance with the energy that moves on Earth; they were the original environmental workers of our species. In the Andes we say that those who still do what they did are the ones doing the work of *Wiracocha*.

Wiraqocha is how we refer to the Divine Source in Andean culture. The name *Wiraqocha* is made out of two words: *wira* and *qocha*. The meaning of *wira* is fat, and the meaning of *qocha* is lake. When we prepare our offerings to feed the Earth, we always put a bit of lama fat in them. Not always but in many instances, we place the fat right in the center of the offering, in the navel, on top of a shell. Fat is life; it is an enormous concentration of vitality. In the offering, the shell is always sitting on a bed of white cotton, which represents a *qocha*, a lake, an abundant source of water and life. Putting these together, it can be said that *Wiraqocha* means "Lake of Vitality" or "Abundant Source of Life and Vitality." As a man of the Andes, in my mental structure the Divine is just that, an abundant source of vitality. To be intelligent and compassionate means to remember to follow the paths by which this vital energy flows, always seeking to nourish the continuity of all life.

I feel so happy when I hear my elders compliment young men and women because they are doing the work of *Wiraqocha*. Anyone can, in his or her own way, do the work of *Wiraqocha* and distribute vitality, nourish what is hungry, raise the vibration of what is too dense or connect masculine and feminine forces to generate more life. These were the tasks of the people who worked in the ancient temples. They received, stored and then distributed the great Universal energy and wisdom that came through the navels of the Earth. They did it so tenderly that the sacred spirits, delighted by the way those ancient humans worked and prayed, shared their power with them. Our ancestors were very powerful people.

CHAPTER THREE

QHAWASHAN

Observing

All the Inca and pre-Inca temples have observation posts. While other functions of ancient temples are now partially or completely damaged, the posts of observation are mostly unchanged and still usable. I have friends who have used them to learn, and I too have used them for my spiritual development.

Understanding the temples as centers of observation can illuminate the methods of ancient people, methods that could be very effective in responding to the severe environmental crisis that threatens the continuity of human life on Earth. An important realization I had while visiting the temples was that the higher or deeper the state of being in the observers, the greater the chance they would discover something useful to improve the life of the people. The temples were built not only to give us opportunities to observe but also to elevate our state of being so we can make more profound observations. In the old days, children and youngsters were not programmed intellectually in the way they are today. Rather they were guided into experiences that helped them become attentive observers eventually capable of unveiling new possibilities and then sharing in the collective responsibility of building a healthy world.

The ancient temples served as schools for the formation of the most advanced and highly developed guardians of life on Earth. The ancient ones constructed numerous observation posts, both within and around each temple, from which apprentices could observe the details of the world. The posts were built in the pathway of the motion of Natures' forces so the apprentices were directly exposed to the energy of what they observed. Looking through a trapezoidal window, or standing in a high spot overlooking a sacred site, they must have felt like fish observing the currents that move them. The vibrations of everything they observed fully entered their body and their being so it wasn't merely their thinking mind interpreting what they saw. The observations were digested by their whole self and were more akin to remembering something familiar than discovering something new. The power of the temple could provoke an altered state in the apprentices, a heightened state of awareness in which they made discoveries. Making a discovery in this case has to do with a magical moment of communication with Nature and the spirit of all things. When the apprentices were ready, it was the Spirits who revealed their secrets to them. Their abilities as mathematicians, artists, farmers, architects, hydraulic engineers, healers or community leaders were activated through these deep practices of observation.

I humbly say that this way of observing is how I learned the little I know. At least it is how I learned to learn. Some indigenous people refer to this type of learning as the practice of receiving original instructions. And I find this expression very accurate because indigenous methodology doesn't try to formulate theories about the true nature of things; rather it lets things tell us what they are. The altered state of mind is key in this methodology. Temples and their altars help us arrive to a lucid state of consciousness where pure listening and deep observation happen effortlessly. We also use medicine plants and various ceremonies to elevate our mind to the heights and depths of the Sacred.

From a very young age, I walked through the temples. While crowds of visitors kept moving from one place to another following a tour guide, the stones told me to stay put, sometimes for hours, in very specific locations from where, over time, I was able to observe the observations of the old sages. First, I allowed myself to be taken to a higher state of consciousness by the power and beauty of what was before me, and then, when I was ready — sometimes much later, sometimes right away — I saw something that made me *remember*. Tears would often flow from my eyes when I realized that this ancient place had been built as a gift for spiritually hungry people like me to learn by unveiling secrets of nature that couldn't be seen in ordinary circumstances. From those experiences I gained more than just knowledge. Downloads of that kind of information leave a mark on you, they build your soul, they shape your mind, they paint the world around you, they change your character and they make you very humble as well as deeply grateful.

On one occasion, I was in Ollantaytambo observing a certain carved stone laying on the ground. After a while, I felt a strong impulse to lay down on it, and I did so. Suddenly, I felt the stone grab my body and I couldn't move. Far from being unpleasant, I felt content and quite sedated. In an instant, I wasn't there anymore. I was in Machu Picchu and there were no tourists but instead indigenous people dressed in the ancient traditional clothes, wearing feathered headdresses and jewelry made of gold. I saw them and they saw me. One of them, a young man with bright eyes, invited me to follow him and showed me around. Everything, be it a tree, a llama, a little plant or stone, was made of gold.

The face of my guide also radiated a soft golden luminescence and seeing his face moved me to tears. The fullness of his contentment and peace radiated toward me, and I felt blessed even though he wasn't trying to bless me. He was simply like that. He was already dead, and more alive than anyone I had ever encountered. Before I returned to the hardness of the stone I was lying on and saw the blue sky above me, my inner being spoke, expressing what it had remembered: there are two Machu Picchus, one is full of tourists and the other is full of spirits.

Four days after this experience, I woke up feeling the building pressure of a thought eager to come to light. I lay in bed a moment before standing up to welcome the thought, which was that no one has found a cemetery near Machu Picchu. Around two thousand people lived there constantly for a few generations and their bones cannot be found. Where did those people go? Nowhere. They are still there, in the other Machu Picchu, the one I saw in my vision.

After participating in so many ceremonies, an experience of that kind is no longer something weird for my mind. I feel comfortable making observations and research in magical states of being. Every time I experience a heightened state of consciousness, sacred spirits are at home in the temple of my mind. Practicing the art of observation, I have learned that our reality is determined not just by the natural and social conditions surrounding us but also by what we choose to focus on. When we focus on something, we give it energy, and it comes to life. I remember, from many years ago, a friend of mine used to carry a gun and precisely because of it attracted criminals. The city where we lived had become too dangerous. In the two years that I worked with him, he had to use his gun to scare away criminals several times. Although we frequented the same neighborhoods, I never needed to use a gun, because I didn't carry one. I was careful and attentive, but not afraid, like someone who had chosen to live in peace. My friend attracted criminals and I didn't. He saw them everywhere while I didn't. By going without a weapon and choosing to cultivate peace, I had to tune into a deep silence and find the guidance I needed to remain safe. In so doing, I always felt led to avoid dangerous situations. Wonderful things happen when we empty our mind and allow the Universe to see through our eyes. Then we see what the Universe sees. The possibilities seen by the Universe through our eyes become activated in our world, and these are usually the best possibilities that exist in the moment to build a more developed, healthy reality. The Universe doesn't have limits; it has infinitely expansive movement; the limits that block us are born from the imagination of a disconnected mind.

The art of building reality through deep

observation is also practiced collectively. There is something extremely powerful about observing someone else observe, which occurs when the members of a group together come into a high state of awareness in a ceremony. People gathered to observe with one another multiply their capacity to uncover precious bits of reality otherwise hidden behind a veil. This collective observing is much like the way light bounces between mirrors facing each other to create a vibrant web of light. An individual standing in a circle during a sacred dance is like one of the mirrors, both receiving and reflecting this web of light and may reach a state of very high consciousness and experience a deep sense of happiness. The heart opens into profound feeling and listening and the mind becomes lucid and bright, seeing the world as wonderful and accepting the responsibility of owning it, of never abandoning what has been seen and recognized. In a circle of observers, this joyous, enlightened feeling is collective and the memory of that intimate experience bonds the people together and helps build community. I have the good fortune of participating in ceremonies where this happens in small groups. And sometimes I wonder how it was when around two thousand people gathered in those big open spaces that exist in the center of sacred sites like Machu Picchu, Caral, or right next to the great pyramids in Egypt. So many people together with a single intention and a single focus of attention:

What did they see while dancing all night under the stars? What did they receive? What did they bring forth into our world?

Generation after generation, it is circles of observers who fuel the ongoing construction of the temples. The circles of observers transcend time. Anyone can go to a temple today and join with the observers of ancient times by standing and observing from the same spots where they stood. In front of these open doors and windows in the temples, some deep aspect of reality, some universal law, some powerful medicine can be seen. New observers make the spiral grow and reinforce a culture rooted in circular development: circular in time, circular in space, and circular in the combined efforts of the people. In indigenous cultures, there are no famous scientists; rather there are generations of community members who together carry the knowledge they all help conceive.

The one who observes is like someone holding a flashlight, illuminating something that was hiding in the dark realm of the unborn. Groups of observers are like constellations of stars that influence everything born under their sign. For centuries, the people of the Andes and the Amazon were under the guidance of the constellation of observers we call our first grandfathers, the founders of our cultures. Every subsequent generation added a new ring to the spiral of the reality first seen by those grandfathers until the day people from another part of the world arrived who couldn't see what we could and ruthlessly crushed all that was sacred for us. By continuing our ceremonies, our generation is doing the best we can to maintain a connection to the memory of our ancestors, keeping alive the habit of receiving sacred instructions from the Earth and the Sky in a modern society that is guided by the limited human mind only.

CHAPTER FOUR

WAK'A

SACRED SITE

One day I was staying in a little town in Peru surrounded by mountains. I was resting in my quiet room right across the street from a plaza when suddenly the church bells began sounding so loudly that my silence was harshly interrupted and a deep sadness arose in me. After the bells stopped, to my surprise the sounds of dozens of *pututos* — traditional Andean trumpets made of conch shells — entered the room and felt like sea waves licking my wounds. Over and over again, the *pututos* made me feel so good that responding to their call I stood up and walked onto the street. Dozens of men and children, who were dressed in colorful traditional clothes and playing their *pututos* under the sun at the front door of the church, melted my heart's hardness and I was able to weep. Following the example of my gentle Andean brothers and sisters, I decided to go inside the church to offer my respects. Sitting there, observing the saints that were gazing at me from the walls, I began to chew some coca leaves I had been carrying in my *ch'uspa*. While taking our Andean sacrament, I prayed to invisible deities that ancient indigenous people secretly placed in the Spanish churches after their traditional temples became part of the spoils of war of the conquistadores. I prayed also to the God of the Catholics; aware that, in truth, there is only one divinity with many different faces. Enlivened with the sweetness of fresh coca leaves dancing in my mouth, my open heart remembered to be grateful for everything that life gives us, and I felt at home.

The Catholic temples now reach high above the plazas of Andean towns, with their bells that call people to gather with God. Our own temples, no longer used for what they were built, preserve a little known history and receive the visit of tourists from all over the world. We call our temples *Wak'a,* sacred site. Before the European invasion, their purpose was to collect and store enormous quantities of vital energy that were infused with cosmic instructions, and this stored sacred power was distributed as needed throughout a vast territory, as both light and food, for the well-being of millions of people.

Large open spaces within the sacred sites allowed large numbers of people to gather. Their prayers, music and dances activated the entire place as a powerful instrument that released high frequency vibrations for the nourishment of life on Earth. Within these sites, certain stones served as antennas for the people and the land to receive information from the grandparents of the Earth: the Sun and other Stars. These stones, named *Wanka,* acted like funnels for cosmic energy to enter the body of Pachamama. A *Wanka* is a standing rock, either with a pointed shape, or more of an egg shape that we see as a womb holding a sacred spirit meant to guide the people and bless the world. In many indigenous societies, standing rocks are held sacred for their connection to the birth of that group's culture. An elder once told me that every time the ancestors chose to settle in a certain area, they first sought a standing rock to serve as the center, or else they placed one. Anchored in the land, this rock informed the powers of Nature that humans were settling in that territory to take their nourishment from it, and to, in return, serve as antennas that connect the land with the Stars.

Later, for fear of their power, Catholic authorities ordered the removal of many standing rocks. In other cases, they built rooms without doors around them, and churches around the rooms. Even though they were hidden behind walls, the *wankas* attracted the indigenous people, who knew they were there, to come to church. Throughout the Andes, many standing rocks are still prisoners under the roofs of Catholic churches. In ancestral times, there were also individuals able to receive the instructions of the Universe and guide their people, so a *Wanka* was not the only antenna in a temple. For centuries, the temples have been deprived of their human antennas as well. The prohibition of indigenous rituals and the imposition of Christian rites meant torture and death for the skilled Andean spiritual workers.

As one of the Andean spiritual workers living in modern times, I feel grateful that my life isn't in danger for being what I was born to be. Things are getting better; but our present is still tainted by a painful past. It is reported that when the first Spaniards arrived at the territories now known as Peru in the sixteenth century, there may have been around twenty million native inhabitants. Fifty years later, only two million remained. This happened in part because of chickenpox brought from Europe and in large part because of edicts signed by the Popes of that time declaring that indigenous peoples of the Americas were not humans but animals and therefore it was permitted that good Christians of Europe take away their temples, lands, and even their lives. Nowadays, we descendants of the survivors are many millions again and we are treated with a new respect and sincere affection by European friends, even though those Papal edicts have never been rescinded.

For centuries, our families have resisted the temptation to harden our hearts, feeling squeezed between two equally damaging alternatives: to be reckless like the conquistadores or to live with the stigma of those who lost their world. Fortunately, we had a third alternative. Thanks to the big hearts of our grandparents, our Andean culture is still very alive, for the resilience and longevity of a nation is not based in military prowess but in its capacity to not lose its tenderness even amidst the cruelest events. The Andean culture is not an angry culture, so our response to all the historic misfortunes that have befallen us is to do as we have always done: sing and dance. We dance with the bells, with the Catholic saints, with the soldiers and the police just as we dance with the spirits of our mountains and the flowers and the little newborn children that lead us to the future. On Christmas day in the city of Cusco, the most beautiful traditional Andean dancers follow behind a band of musicians in and out of the Cathedral, singing and dancing. The leaders of every community that come to this celebration walk ahead of the dancers carrying a little box with a figure of a newborn boy surrounded by maize and flowers. The dancers, gorgeously adorned with flowers and feathers and full of vitality, leap around Cusco's main square singing:

"*Waylia, Waylia, Waylia!*" -an old warrior call now used to ignite the heart's fierce determination to continue living. The female dancers wear colorful Andean skirts shaped like mountains along with Spanish-style hats. The male dancers wear traditional Andean clothing from the waist up and the leather boots and riding pants of a Spanish landowner. As is clearly shown by this folk dress, rather than rejecting the invading presence our ancestors absorbed it and danced with it, and we are still dancing with it.

Thanks to a sacred quality we call *Munay* that lives in the human heart, the spirit and dignity of people who were mercilessly mistreated are still intact and dancing. *Munay* is the energy of the will of the heart and what moves love into action. It is our profound love for all life that allows us to include and accept everything, even those who have deeply hurt us, as part of the beautiful world we care for so dearly. Even when the ancient treasures of our country, the jungles, rivers and mountains are desecrated every day, sometimes with the collaboration of our own relatives who are desperate for money, most Andean people still carry a smile as wide as a sunrise. In fact, we even feel grateful for the last five hundred years of painful difficulties because it has all helped us learn that as long as we don't lose our hearts, all that our hearts have always loved remains ours. Precisely because we haven't lost our hearts, we remain available to someday continue what was interrupted.

In the society where I grew up, the primary collective emotion was a sort of outer resignation coupled with an underlying unspoken hope that something really good would one day come. We have waited hundreds of years and remain hopeful for its arrival. Pachamama changes periodically, and we knew that one day the winds would blow again in favor of our heart-centered, Earth-loving culture. Many signs tell us the time has arrived. Among those signs is the amount of people from all over the world coming to visit who are truly interested in the wisdom of our ancestors. Our spiritual ways are again in high demand, now permitted and respected in a way they weren't just forty or fifty years back.

Another sign is the emergence of a powerful natural event that was prophesized long ago. This is the rapid ascension of the vibrational frequency of all life forms on Earth, clearly perceived as a new reality by intuitive women and spiritually awake children as well as by spiritual workers called Paq'o, Pampamisayuq, Altomisayuq, or shamans by modern people. While most of humanity is still unaware of it, some of us are trying to not miss the opportunity and take advantage of this high energy in motion that supports the re-emergence of the best of the human spirit.

Like any other living creature, the Earth grows.

Through the power of our ceremonies, we can perceive how earthly life forms are suddenly vibrating at a much higher frequency and coming into a more refined form of existence, increasing their power. This increase in quality of energy is now possible for all that inhabits the Earth, including human beings. We are all invited to move to a higher vibrational frequency that promotes greater vitality, higher consciousness, and more joyous existence. Unfortunately, we are being too slow at accepting this invitation because of the fact that modern human beings have lost much of their capacity to receive original instructions. Compared with other life forms that live on Earth, they are not easily guided by Universal Powers such as the Sun and Moon and Cosmic Winds. Most of humanity continues to follow the man-made instructions of the officially sanctioned education and belief systems of this era.

All human beings could have arrived to the high frequency of the present time just as the little river pebbles have, but we are lagging behind because the work of our spiritual growth begun by our wise ancestors all over the world was interrupted some time ago. It was interrupted when the temples — the navel temples, the heart temples, the antenna temples, the sacred agriculture temples, the original university temples, and the tribal way of life temples — were invaded, damaged and eventually closed.

In Cusco, a city shaped as a Puma, the head of the Puma was once a temple that served as an antenna from which the Inca community drew their thoughts and their rain. The ceremonial area there is called Saqsaywaman, a magnificent place that dazzles people with its enormous perfectly cut stones placed like pieces of a puzzle without mortar to form the beautiful zigzagged walls of its main structure. When the conquistadores overtook the area, their political and religious authorities forced the local people to destroy parts of this sacred temple and then transport some of those huge stones down the hill to construct the Cathedral of Cusco, built directly on top of another destroyed Incan temple called Siwarkancha. In a similar way, many, many temples were violated and damaged and thousands of years of human development were instantly severed, interrupted and abandoned. Temples in the Andean world such as Saqsaywaman, Ollantaytambo, Chavin, Kalasasaya and many others were intentionally left broken and deprived of their sacred equipment. The same has occurred around the world in places like Stonehenge, Teotihuakan, Tikal, Chichen-Itza, Luxor, Philae, Loughcrew — the list is endless. Now tourists, who admire them as relics of the past, visit these places unable to remember them as homes of the ancient human spirit. Built strong enough to remain intact up to our time, with the proper maintenance all of them could still be doing their crucial work of helping humanity stay connected to the instructions of the Universe like an infant to the mother's milk. In the present time, they could connect us to the cosmic forces guiding the increase of the vibrational frequency of life on Earth.

For centuries, the religious authorities of the colonizers didn't continue the work for the ascension of the human race, nor did they allow us to do so. Otherwise we would already be enjoying a feeling of spiritual and human elevation instead of continually worrying about what may happen to our lands, waters and our children's lives if the Earth doesn't heal soon. The human amnesia that has allowed our natural sources of life to be mistreated and become contaminated is something we see as the consequence of five hundred years of not doing enough of the sacred human work. Now the time to continue what was interrupted is arriving, and we have much catching up to do, much to heal and much to rebuild.

Something difficult for us to face is that our ancient temples are still called ruins. The minds of the people we descend from were wired in the same way temples were designed, so to call our temples ruins is to say the same about our ancient Andean mind. Living now in a time of great opportunity, a time when the light has returned to guide the new ascension of the human spirit, we find ourselves wanting to be ready, wanting to rebuild our temple, trying to accept, with some difficulty, the beauty of what we really are. Loud voices tell us that being wise and healthy is for us a matter of the past, and that now we must follow the proposals of the developed countries of the modern world. But Andean people can still walk over mountaintops for days without hiding from the cold and Amazonian people through the thick jungle in the dark, shoeless and without a flashlight, so I have no doubt that we have the strength to continue, in some new way, what was interrupted.

CHAPTER FIVE

LAKOTA

FRIEND

The sacred way of life of many tribes in North America was also interrupted. One tribe that I am very familiar with is the Lakota, as I have spent many years of my life participating in their most sacred ceremonies. I am grateful to them for their generous sharing, for giving me what I needed to live a life focused on prayer and based on sacred principles. For many years, I have followed the lead of my adopted father, Basil Brave Heart, and it has never been difficult to integrate his teachings and example with my strong Andean heart.

Just as my ancestors of the Andes found the center of their world in powerful places like Lake Titiqaqa, Cusco or Chavin, the Black Hills of South Dakota were and still are the highest sacred lands of the Lakota people. *Paha Sapa,* the Black Hills, are deeply revered and respected by many indigenous tribes as the site of important annual ceremonies in generations past. These mountains stand as the location of the umbilicus through which the Universal Mother spiritually and physically nourished all aspects of the Lakota sacred way of life. By contrast, American entrepreneurs viewed the Black Hills as merely a vast gold mine and that view was shared by the U.S. government and defended by its army.

The trouble all began with a white man crossing Lakota territory who lost his cow. When Lakota warriors, who lived in a sacred world of opportunities and relationships and had no concept of private proprietorship, saw a wandering cow, they deemed it a gift from the Earth and killed it for meat. The cow's owner, by contrast, lived in a human centered world of possessions and laws and couldn't afford to lose his animal. If he had approached the hunters to address the issue, it would have resulted in a shared feast and exchanged gifts; but instead he complained to the soldiers at the nearest fort. The collision of these two worlds on a fateful day in 1854 was truly explosive.

At that time, the treaty that granted the Lakota (Sioux) Tribe a vast territory around the Black Hills, extending from South and North Dakota to parts of Nebraska and Wyoming, had not been yet violated by the U.S. Government. This treaty also granted permission to settlers and merchants traveling west to cross Lakota territory without being attacked. When the cow's owner found out his animal was hunted, he accused the Lakota of stealing and destroying his property. A group of soldiers was sent to arrest the hunters but, unaware of any transgression, the Lakota refused to be taken into custody and further rejected the authority of soldiers in their native homelands. So after the soldiers attacked and killed one of the most respected elders in the Lakota encampment, a man named Conquering Bear, the Lakota braves took the lives of the whole regiment.

As history tells, this incident was followed by a sequence of battles in which honorable and brave men like Crazy Horse, Sitting Bull, Red Cloud, Spotted Tail, Black Thunder, American Horse, Men Afraid of His Horses, and many others won battles against the U.S. Army but ended up losing the larger war, one in which the Lakota faced insurmountable odds. When the conflicts ended, the entrepreneurs took enormous bounty: free access to the gold in the Black Hills and abundant land for their cows. One hundred and fifty years have passed since the U.S. government took the Black Hills, and gold is still being extracted. Meanwhile, the descendants of the Lakota people first placed on reservations continue to endure some of the most difficult conditions of life, even in one of the materially wealthiest countries in the world.

When the Lakota people were forced to abandon their nomadic ways and traditional culture and adapt to living on contained reservations, their youth were separated from their families. They were sent to boarding schools where their long hair — the outer manifestation of their spirit — was cut off, and they were not allowed to speak the Lakota language, prohibited from practicing their ancient ceremonies, ridiculed as savages when they exhibited the typical traits of Earth People, and were Western educated and Christianized.

The way I heard my elder Basil Brave Heart explain it, the Lakota people were very confused by these newcomers whose language and worldview put too many fences around everything tangible and intangible: their ranches, their houses, their chickens, as well as their beliefs and thoughts. The boarding schools were designed to give the Lakota that same compartmentalized mind, one full of fences separating the different pieces of reality. The indigenous children were conditioned to no longer see the world from a wide, inclusive perspective but from a narrow, single-focused lens that always separated *that over there* from *this over here*. From then on, the understanding of the world had to be composed of rigid concepts approved by the intellectual authorities of the colonizers and could no longer be the product of a direct connection with a changing reality that has clarity as well as mysteries.

We are what we eat. The people who historically ate the strong, wild buffalo that could never be fenced enjoyed the freedom of immense physical landscapes as well as vast mental territories in which everything was known to be sacred, related, and interconnected and where understanding came from putting together, in an immediate encompassing awareness, all that was perceived, felt and thought. When living in the wild, it is easy to perish at any time and there is not much time to process events. Your mind has to be fast, decisive, and guided by the wisdom of shared experience. Because all Lakota shared that type of mind, communication among the people remained simple without much need to over-explain or over-analyze anything or figure out from the start how something would end.

The Lakota maintained a heart-centered and spiritually guided culture, and the methodology of the heart is simple: you feel you know something from a deep place within and let this knowing guide your actions without hesitation or doubt. In such a culture, like the buffalo, the people keep moving forward together even when a big storm approaches. The heart also guides you to take care of relationships along the way so that you never end up walking alone, like the owner of the cow that started the war. That white man, a good person for certain, must have roamed the lush

Black Hills and enjoyed the most beautiful nights, gifted with much time to silently observe the stars. But it is possible he couldn't truly see or hear them and that he wasn't open in his heart. Instead, he may have lain under his blanket at night embracing his rifle, scared by any noise, afraid of losing his life or his cow, waiting for the night to end quickly. He may have been unable to be oriented by the sacred powers, finding himself alone because, in his culture, it was not appropriate to make friends with the sacred spirits of the land; that was a fence he couldn't cross.

Our cultures always had their own mental fences, composed of taboos and behavioral restrictions meant to organize the communitarian life; but none of them impeded the mental and spiritual expansiveness of an individual. In present times, many Lakota people, Andean people and descendants from many different tribes face a multitude of new fences that cannot be crossed, invisible borders enforced by the norms of a colonized society as well as by religion and the trends of modern culture. Even what we eat on a daily basis has been fenced, treated, packaged and labeled, so what feeds our body and our vitality carries the restricted nature of those plants and animals turned into products. For the most part, a large number of indigenous people no longer eat what carries the energy of the expansive wilderness. Instead of powerful, nomadic, environmentally friendly wild buffalos, most Native peoples in North America eat the meat of cows raised in fenced ranches. They have been misguided to live in a way that creates huge environmental imbalances that will greatly affect their future generations. On top of this, most of today's Native youth are no longer concerned about how well they eat or protect the Earth that produces their food. Most of the healthiest young people are hoping to receive a "superior education" that results in abandoned farms, hunting grounds and ceremonial lodges.

Having spent centuries dealing with the maneuvers of colonization, we indigenous people now feel a need to dissolve the fences and re-indigenize ourselves in connection to the very ancient ways that were common to all tribes and indigenous nations. In the past, we fought to maintain our traditions in order not to lose our culture to an invading presence and not have others dictate how we should live. Today the motivation is changing, as many of us are expressing our desire to become self-sufficient again, to employ ancient methods of sustainability because the world that has tried to educate us has proven unable to sustain life. The multitudes of cows overgrazing, the endless mining of sacred metals and the ubiquity of modern technology are all destroying our natural world. Instead of continuing to believe we must become educated in the ways of the modern world in order to adapt to a high-tech future, we can instead reorient ourselves to our lands and utilize the adaptation methods of our ancestors. Their very effective methods depended on a certain way of using the mind and the heart that allowed them to connect all aspects of reality, creating unity in their world, accessing the most profound truths through a simple, open and practical way of thinking.

As a Peruvian who grew up surrounded by ancient sacred sites, I have often wondered if one day our broken temples will be rebuilt. Who knows; perhaps someday this will happen but I may not live to see it. What I see happening in my time is that many of us, Lakota, Andean and many others want to repair the broken temple of our minds, to pick up precious forgotten pieces and dissolve all unnecessary fences. Some sacred power is instructing us to move freely within our minds as we look for our true selves. Many of us now seek to identify and release the colonization in our thinking, to revitalize our native languages and once again listen to our elders. Listening to our wisest elders has become an urgent need. We still have a few holy men and holy women who grew up when the mindset of the modern world wasn't as pervasive as it is nowadays. These old people are dying quickly, and we may be the last generation with a chance to listen to the wisdom they carry in their memory. We can give them the opportunity to pass on what has been passed on for thousands of years but could soon be forgotten.

Paradoxically, what the modern world tried to take away from our elders when they were young and forcibly educated in the "civilized" ways of the Christian European culture is now in high demand. The damage inflicted to our dear Mother Earth is making people from all heritages recognize that our ancient ways are a treasure that should not be lost and instead used for resolving the current problems of human societies, very serious problems such as the impending crisis regarding water. People from all over the world now seek out those who still carry the ancient wisdom of humanity aligned with Nature. Those of us with the great privilege of having elders who still remember the sacred way of life are the ones who know how to respect these living treasures. We know to refrain from looking in their eyes when they speak and instead gaze at their hands, observing the wrinkles, the markings and pathways left by the sacred energy that passed through them, unfenced and unstoppable, when they worked and when they prayed and asked for help, humbly touching the ground or extending their arms towards the sky. So I pray with gratitude for the health and happiness of my elders, one of them being a generous and kind Lakota holy man named Basil Brave Heart.

CHAPTER SIX

WILKA QORAKUNA

SACRED PLANTS

In our traditional temples, the position of the doors and windows and the arrangement of all the rooms are key to the way energy moves within them, and the way energy moves is key to the generation of sacred power by the temple. It is the same in the temple of our mind. The structure of our mind enables earthly and cosmic energies to circulate in a way that they become potentiated to the point of illumination, or the opposite can also be true. Our mind can serve as a basket of obstacles that constantly blocks the circulation of light. One may want to be compassionate with others or help heal the environment, but if the mind isn't a well-built temple, wisdom cannot flow through it. A simple way to check if the mind is putting up obstacles or allowing the circulation of light is to test our capacity to listen.

The Kogi people of the Sierra Nevada de Santa Marta in Colombia are masters in the art of keeping the temple of the mind well built. They honor clear, simple thinking as an integral part of their culture. The Kogi live in a remote and inaccessible land and thus are among the least damaged by the waves of colonization that passed through South America. They are widely considered as some of the wisest people on Earth and are referred to as the "Older Brothers" of the human species. One of their spiritual leaders, a *Mamo*, once delivered a message to the modern world in which he stated that, "Our thinking creates the world. Modern man needs to learn how to think better thoughts or the world will be destroyed." He then clarified that, in his culture, "To think is to listen."

When I heard this *Mamo* state that thinking is equal to listening, I realized how terrible, and yet how commonplace, it is for us to think without listening. When we do this, we must sound like musicians who play without hearing the other players: self-absorbed, locked in bubbles, listening only to ourselves, believing we are making music when in truth we are merely allowing the ego to make lots of noise. According to the Kogi, this noise destroys the world. Out of my love for this Earth, I choose to remain humble and listen as much as I can.

In order to heal or renew our capacity to listen,

indigenous people have always called upon the help of those who are great listeners and are like living antennas. Some of these are spiritually gifted humans and others come from Nature, most especially the medicine plants. Since ancient times, Pachamama has put plants within our reach that help us clean and rewire our mind and remove the mental fences that impede deep listening. With the help of these sacred medicine plants, all indigenous nations have developed rituals to continually renew our intelligence.

As Andean people, like the Kogi, we too have learned not to think alone, and to always have someone that we can listen to in those moments when our mind seeks understanding. We learned from our grandparents to think with the coca leaves, to think with tobacco, to think with waterfalls, with trees, with the spirits of mountains, with lakes, with the sacred spirits that our prayers call. This is a sharp ancient way of using the mind that leads me to never act on my own, to never shape or influence the world without listening to the voices of the Earth, expressed through birds, winds, thunders and all kinds of visits that always arrive in the precise moment.

For our modern side, thinking is about the intellectual capacity to draw from our own baggage in order to elaborate smart and convincing statements; for our indigenous side thinking has more to do with the capacity to receive and digest sacred instructions. When thinking, we remember to activate our antennas because we could be seriously wrong if we think without listening to original instructions.

From the moment a signal is sent to our mind by the Earth or the Universe, and until it becomes energy that fuels our actions, it travels through many parts of the temple of our being, some physical, some emotional and others intellectual. All these parts of us have to listen, and in the end, once there are no mental fences interrupting the flow of information, all of them accept the instruction from the sources of life in unison. As complex as it sounds, this process of receiving and following instructions is very simple. A human being may naturally experience it many times a day, just as mountains, animals and plants do. Mountains have big bellies, so their digestive system needs a good deal of time to put the energy they receive from the cosmos into circulation on Earth. Animals, like us, also need a little time to digest cosmic light, but plants can move the energy very quickly. Plants immediately transform the cosmic frequency of the information they receive from the sunlight into an earthly frequency. This is why the relationship with edible and medicine plants is the backbone of indigenous cultures. Plants are some of the most revered and respected allies of our peoples.

In the Sierra Nevada, Kogi men carry handwoven

bags full of sweet coca leaves as they walk. It is customary that every time they meet one another, whether casually or in a formal encounter, they exchange some leaves, each person pulling a handful from his bag to put in the other's bag. This ritual invites a moment of communication with the spirit of the Earth that lives in the coca leaves. The invitation is to think, together and with her, even when no words are exchanged. This sacred communication is an act of communion; it is a sacrament and they do it every day, many times a day.

In Andean towns, we do something similar. To chew coca leaves in silence before sharing words prepares us to really listen. We walk carrying coca leaves in our *ch'uspa,* and when we visit with others who live in a traditional way everyone pulls out some leaves, spreads them out upon a colorful manta and the sharing begins. As the leaves are passed among us, a profound silence opens up, one spacious enough for the mountains, rivers, birds and ancestors to be present. We too become really present when we hand someone coca leaves with tenderness.

In Iquitos, Pucallpa, Tarapoto and other areas of the Amazon jungle, women roll small cigars with pure unmodified tobacco called *Mapacho.* These *Mapacho* cigars are not smoked just for pleasure; they are used for prayer, to think by listening. Prayer is essentially a form of communication, a way of letting the sacred universal powers know that we need help and that our antennas are ready to receive. By smoking *Mapacho,* we communicate with Pachamama in her jungle form, and the jungle is wise beyond what we could ever imagine. When smoking this tobacco, I think better thoughts. Through the tobacco, the spirit of the jungle has often spoken to me with the voices of Sacred Spirits that live suspended in the crevices of waterfalls, of wise snakes that carry the vitality of humid soil, of powerful medicine plants that offer themselves in dreams when we need help, of jaguar elders that show the way through the dark, and of wise pink dolphins that are always playing. When I smoke *Mapacho,* the water in my mouth is touched by the memory of the rain that fell upon the plant while she grew in the jungle, and then this water flows through my body. It helps me to remember. As I remember the power and beauty of our Mother, I feel the jungle people's nocturnal symphony resonate in my blood and bring me back to a very humble place where I can sing that jungle song I am hearing, an authentic, eternal song that belongs not to me but to all life.

In many parts of the world it has become difficult for the common citizen to find unmodified tobacco, the one good for true listening. In the United States it is illegal for the common farmer to grow tobacco. Apart from the companies that mix it with chemicals to make harmful cigarettes, only indigenous tribes can grow medicinal tobacco freely on their lands. This implies an underlying lack of permission for non-tribal people to be indigenous to this Earth and use her plants to listen to her, to think with her. Many brave people do it despite the obstacles but, for the most part, sacred plants are used by so called non-indigenous people only for recreation or self-medication and without the wisdom of the ancient rituals that give knowledge of the right quantities of medicine, the right timing for their use, and the way of opening an intimate relationship with the plant's spirit. Many of those brave relatives without an indigenous tribe are dedicated to changing the harmful social and economic structures and are constantly defending the environment, the endangered wild creatures and the oppressed people. Yet how can they receive all the guidance and instructions they need when it isn't permissible for them to use the medicines of the Earth, and when they are not given the knowledge of how to use them properly?

The world greatly needs leaders and workers who can listen; but wise communication rituals do not exist in settings where important decisions that influence the state of the world are made. We have only a short time to make changes for the healing and recovery of the environment; therefore, listening to the instructions of the Earth and the Universe is now crucial. The Earth and the Universe are billions of years old and they already know what we humans are painfully trying to figure out. We are not foreigners visiting the Earth or the Universe; we are part of them, we belong to their great bodies just like cells belong to ours, so knowing how to listen to their guidance is essential. Unfortunately, in today's world when a group of well-intentioned people gather to discuss an important issue, we cannot take for granted that we are listening as we think together; we may instead be wasting precious time. It depends completely on the state of our being, on how quiet, open and tender we are in the moment. It depends on how humble we are even as we seek to wield power to affect change. Listening deeply, we can be moved to a different frequency. Getting away from our habitual mental and emotional frequencies is already the creation of change. As our mind moves into unknown territory, our understanding naturally expands and we become able to make a discovery, like an open-minded child.

The modern world has produced wonders that we all enjoy. It is a pleasure to watch a movie on a high definition screen or to ride a motorcycle. The problem is humanity created the modern world without listening to the Earth. She was never asked if it would harm her body if oil were extracted, or if her pure air wanted to be polluted with smoky emissions, or if her plants wanted to drink pesticides. When furniture production for human comfort became industrialized, the trees were not asked if they liked chainsaws or agreed to die en masse for the cause. When plastic became so convenient that endless items were formed from it, we never asked the Earth or the whales if they wanted to have this invasive element stuck in their arteries. When cities grew to huge dimensions and plumbing systems allowed people to easily obtain water and take as many baths as they wanted, water wasn't asked if she could stay vital inside pipes. As these technological advancements gave us humans so much power over the Earth's elements and increased our comfort and safety, to ask these questions and listen for the answers seemed ridiculous. But today, seeing the devastation caused by climate change, many people realize that to ask the Earth isn't a bad idea; modern people just don't know how to do that. Were those who developed the technologies and industries that shaped the modern world really thinking?

The people of the ancient Paracas Culture of the southern coast of Peru knew about the need to "cut off their head" in order to think well. In their tapestries and ceramics, the sacred grandfather of our race, *Apu Kon Titi Wiraqocha*, is often depicted as a man flying with a heart in the place of his head and a little cut-off head carried in his hand. Some anthropologists have interpreted this icon as a representation of a warrior God who beheaded his enemies, but the interpretation from the Andean cultural perspective is that the man "beheaded" himself in order to become wise. He put his heart where his head had been making himself capable of thinking and feeling simultaneously, which is a way of thinking by listening. Activating this personal sacred power was the most difficult initiation of the ancient warriors who loved the Earth and their people so much that they were willing to die before their death. They renounced being the one who knows everything and is always right in order to make space for the emergence of the one who listens. It is well known that spiritual workers of ancient Andean cultures put weights on their ears to elongate them, and were known as the "long ears". They were very respected by the people of their time because of their capacity to listen. In their actions, they were able to match the concepts articulated in their language with the states of being they had mastered through their spiritual discipline. And then they didn't need to talk much about what had to be done; rather, they were the living expression of what needed to be done.

CHAPTER SEVEN

MOSQOKUSHAN

DREAMING

I was a tall, strong Samurai sitting on a white horse, looking at a wolf as white as the moon that was crossing the path right in front of me. With great speed and precision, I pulled a knife from under my belt and threw it. The knife entered deeply into the flesh beneath the ribs, and the last image I saw, before waking up, was the white wolf lying dead, its belly stained bright red with blood.

Some dreams are not easy to interpret, and this was one of those dreams. It took me a while to be sure that the few cups of Guayusa tea I had after waking up had given me some medicine for interpreting dreams. My mind, while physically sober as is always the case after drinking Guayusa tea, surprisingly became filled with what I perceived as snake medicine. Out of the blue, I started thinking about snakes and even saw them when I closed my eyes. So I decided to take advantage of this visit and prayed to the sacred snake to help me interpret the dream with her wisdom. As a result, I ended up feeling only deep frustration. No interpretation I tried to make had the flavor of a real spiritual insight. I even considered having been wrong about my tea having snake medicine in it, and enjoyed laughing at myself. But when I stood and went to work in the garden it became clear that the tea had mysteriously put snake medicine in my body. So much medicine that perhaps a big snake slept all night with her body lying alongside the plant whose leaves were in my tea.

Knowing how easy it is to injure one's back when pushing a wheelbarrow that carries too much weigh, I did it anyway. As I moved forward pushing all that weight, I came to a very rugged downhill slope and the wheelbarrow twisted in a violent way that for a moment made me consider letting it drop to protect my back. Surprisingly, my body instead chose to relax and moved as a graceful dancer. Instantly, my hips loosened up like when playing soccer and I was able to keep the wheelbarrow upright and moving forward at high speed. It felt so good! I immediately attributed my body's skill to the snake's medicine, so I stopped and sat down to give thanks. The dirt in the wheelbarrow next to me, a bit wet, had a familiar smell that made me smile because it reminded me that the Earth is a woman. As I sat there, smelling wet dirt and looking at the sky, I appreciated that the office where I work has no walls. Many of my friends who are dedicated servants of the Earth and humanity, people on the front line of the effort to improve life on our planet, work in offices all day surrounded by walls instead of dirt and sky, interacting with phones and computers instead of mosquitos, birds, talking winds and messenger plants. What I wish for those friends is lots of Pachamama, meaning lots of time and space, with much less hurry and more time to experience sacred silly moments like the one I was having while sitting on the dirt trying to interpret a powerful dream.

The moment I needed her, the snake helped me not to hurt my back. And then she also helped me interpret my dream. After the snake medicine from a simple cup of Guayusa tea awakened in my body while I pushed the wheelbarrow, the meaning of my dream suddenly became clear: the white wolf was the moon and I had made the moon bleed. The blood pouring from the wolf's belly was the most vivid image in my dream, the one that lingered in my mind. The following day my interpretation was confirmed when my wife Marilyn told me there was a lunar eclipse happening that morning, one that makes the moon look red, a powerful cosmic event called a "Blood Moon." How did I dream about the Blood Moon twenty-four hours before it happened when no one had told me about it? Someone or something must have talked to my body, to my deepest mind, most probably Father Sun. In my dream I wasn't merely aware of the Blood Moon that would happen a day later, but I literally felt the sensation of triggering this event with a strong surge of male energy as if I were the Sun. In my dream, I participated in the cosmic event. I was one with the Sun!

It was important for me to learn the timing of the eclipse, because it had a strong influence on my wife's state of being as well as mine that week. Knowing that a strong cosmic energy was affecting us helped us stay calm and cautious. Speaking about my dream gave us the grounding to live the next few days under the influence of the eclipse without losing our balance.

The open mind that knows things, that is directly informed by the Universal Powers without having to think in a linear way, can orient us in our life and in our work. Some people refer to this as dreaming when it happens while asleep and as intuition when it occurs while awake. In my childhood I learned that intuition is not a rare psychic ability, it is Nature talking to our body and is an inherent quality all of us have and can use. When practiced regularly, as most indigenous people do, we become accustomed to our Mother Pachamama and other natural powers keeping us well informed, even in the midst of tremendous chaos. To have a humble mind free of toxins gives us the capacity to listen, really listen, and become capable of receiving the instructions we need.

The first time I tasted Guayusa tea I was in the jungle of Ecuador with the beautiful people of the Sapara tribe. Each morning long before dawn when it was still dark, a group of men lit a fire and placed a big pot filled with water and lots of Guayusa leaves on top of it. By the time everyone in the camp woke up the tea was ready, and we all gathered to drink it together and share our dreams. The tea gave us the medicine needed to end our dreamtime and fully awaken. It also enhanced our ability to remember and articulate our dreams, which we all did aloud, receiving the help of the most experienced interpreters of the tribe, my friend Manari among them. The Sapara, like the people of many other Amazonian tribes, do this every morning of their lives, together discovering how the day will go by looking at the opportunities and warnings presented in their dreams.

I wonder what guidance the Sapara people are receiving from their dreaming these days after their government gave oil companies permits to drill in their tribal territories. Something that was very clear for centuries has now become unclear: Who is the owner of that jungle? Is it the government? Is it the oil company? Is it the tribe? Is it the jaguar?

Big machines could soon arrive and begin killing huge numbers of trees and animals and poison the soil and rivers. Like gods, the newcomers will expel beautiful people from an earthly paradise. Soon after, trucks will motor through the newly opened roads with loads of sweets and alcohol to help the locals forget the pain, and later missionaries will come to save their conflicted souls from the "evil" of living as traditional indigenous people. After a couple generations, they will be thought of only as farmers because their old way of life will have disappeared. The corporations will have reaped a triple reward: reducing the number of Earth People who stand up for the rights of the environment against commercial interests, receiving huge monetary profits from the resources extracted from the tribe's territory, and creating a new base of addicted customers who have forgotten the old ways or never knew them. All this is just about to happen or not - hopefully not.

CHAPTER EIGHT

PAMPAMISAYUQ

THE ONE WHO HAS
THE HEART OF THE TERRITORY

In the Andes, we are aware that seeds contain the genetic memory of the Universe and therefore to us they are more valuable than gold. We are very clear that, as Earth People, we are the owners of seeds. When they receive the magic touch of water, the seeds activate their memory and open a cycle of growth that develops them into ripe nourishment for the continuity of life. They become food for those hungry today and produce new seeds for those who will be hungry tomorrow. Plants that we eat regularly, grown from pure seeds, feed us with all the proteins, vitamins, minerals and other nutrients contained in them, and they also feed us with the talent of the seeds. To carry the memory of all that the Universe has learned through its total experience is the talent of seeds. The Universal memory we ingest through our food allows us to participate in the development of Universal Life, to belong to it by sharing in its intelligence, its sacred motion, and its ability to reproduce and thrive generation after generation. This is the original democracy. It is our birthright to have access to information broadcasted by the Universe for the benefit of all, and this is what seeds provide to us.

When I spoke about this with a Peruvian sage named Mario Osorio, he told me that when the plants in my farm are developing, their leaves are ears listening to the Sun speak, updating them about current universal events, especially those that influence the present state of life on Earth. Those of us who eat the plants receive the updates as well and this is how our bodies are given the necessary instructions to adapt to the changes in the environment where we live.

But what happens when the plants we eat are genetically modified? Those plants do not come from seeds carrying the memory of the Universe but from seeds that have been altered with information imprinted by human beings focused on the goals and needs of mass production and successful commerce. The leaves of the plants that are not allowed to reproduce naturally have their original nature blocked. They cannot receive updates from the Sun and, in turn, the updates will not be given to the animals and people that eat these plants nor will they reside in the new seeds produced by these plants. It is fair to say that the culture of genetically modified food unplugs humans from our direct connection to the guidance of the Universe. This precious guidance is meant to land in our bodies whenever we eat to help us adapt to the changing conditions of life on Earth.

A culture that accepts genetically modified organisms (GMOs) in its food dissolves the original democracy that gave every form of life access to the essential information moving between the cosmos and the Earth. But Monsanto did not create this culture where humans live disconnected from the guidance of the Universe. Monsanto and other companies simply took advantage of a human tendency of extreme spiritual forgetfulness already in motion for generations. The social conditions to support a culture of genetic modification existed long before GMO plants were grown. In a way, some portion of humanity became genetically modified even before the plants did by losing the sense of being indigenous, of belonging to the Earth. Seeds were lost only after people lost their most valuable inheritance - the memory of their ancestors. When humans, especially those in Europe, ceased to act like Earth People, when they stopped thinking with plants and listening to the Earth and the Sky, they were no longer informed by the real sources of news.

Historically, by force and not by choice, beautiful ancient human cultures that were also guided by uncorrupted sages and the collective wisdom of humble community councils became brutally repressed. Organized religions and militarized political authorities enforced their false notion of a perfect society, one comprised of controlled, subservient people. These new authorities refined the skills of linear reasoning to always find rational justifications for their unjust actions and dismissed all manner of previously honored feelings, intuitive insights and direct spiritual guidance. They forced people to be educated in their model of rationality, and the people became accustomed to receiving instructions only from human authorities and no longer from the Earth or the Universe or any authentic spiritual sources. Along the way, masses of people were subjugated and lost ownership of their wild hearts and minds, and in many cases their land and crops as well. Thus, many years later when a few companies claimed to be the owners of the precious seeds that carry the memory of the Universe, there were too many people who passively accepted.

In Peru, a strong movement of resistance took place. Organizations of farmers and one of the best chefs in our country led a major protest that successfully forced the Peruvian government to ban the production and cultivation of GMO seeds. The people of thirty-seven other countries have also pressed their governments to pass laws forbidding GMO food, relying on the results of scientific studies to validate their case. It is interesting that our so-called uneducated Andean people did not need scientific studies to know that GMO seeds run counter to the continuity of life. Andean farmers who haven't lost their indigenous mind and heart have always remembered that seeds are more valuable than gold. Even when Spanish-descended landlords became the legal proprietors of enormous portions of land taken by the conquistadores, the indigenous people of the Andes, together with their allies in the natural and spiritual worlds, never lost true ownership of what they loved the most: their mountains, lakes and rivers, and beloved seeds. The new authorities could never tame or annihilate the real owner that lived within thousands of Andean and Amazonian people, and still exists somewhere inside every human: an undomesticated, original, wild creature, a fierce protector of life with a tender heart, wisely disguised as a lady or a gentleman.

According to indigenous thought, the corporations that produce GMO seeds do not have a heart like the one of humans, bears, pumas and all the wild guardians of natural spaces. Therefore they are not capable of being good "owners" of anything alive. In our Indigenous cultures, we have a different notion of "ownership."

One day I arrived with a group of people from the United States to the Sapara people's lands in the middle of the Amazon jungle in Ecuador. As soon as we arrived to the area designated for our camp, the tribe's men told us emphatically not to be afraid at night because they had already talked to the owner. "He was walking around here yesterday," the oldest man said, "We told him you were coming and asked permission for you to camp in this place. Don't worry about anything. The owner is happy you are here." The American woman beside me, totally confused, whispered in my ear, "Who is he talking about? Who is the owner of this jungle?" I responded, "He is talking about a jaguar that came through this area last night."

For the indigenous mind, everything that exists has an owner. But an owner is not a proprietor; it is more like a guardian. It always startles me to hear people speak about the land they inhabit as "my property" or even "the property." In Runasimi, we just add the suffix "*yuq*" to any word and it means we are referring to "the one who has it." For example, *wasi* means house, and *wasiyuq* means the owner of the house. However, the suffix *yuq* does not imply that the house is someone's personal property. It just tells us that someone has it, that there is one who has an intimate relationship with the house, who both uses it and cares for it.

One mountain in the Andes is named *Phaqchayuq*.

Phaqcha means waterfall so *Phaqchayuq* means "the one that has the waterfall." In the rainy season, this mountain has a waterfall in it; but the waterfall is not the property of the mountain, the mountain simply holds and shelters the waterfall. Someone who has been given the responsibility of carrying a sacred altar, which is an instrument to communicate with the spirit world, is called *Misayuq*. *Misa* means altar, so the word *Misayuq* is understood as, "the one who has the altar and is responsible for carrying and protecting it."

Yoga practitioners know the word Yoga comes from the Sanskrit word *yug*, which means "to link or join together." I was told the practice of Yoga aims to create energetic links between different parts of the body so a person becomes internally integrated. In essence, the Runasimi suffix *yuq* expresses the same thing. In Andean thought, ownership is not about possession; it is about developing a strong link with someone or something. In our culture, to have a deep bond with anything alive, be it human, animal, plant, land, water, wind, fire, or spirit, makes us its "parents" or "owners." We deeply care for all that we become linked to, and this creates unity in our world. Through "ownership" we become "glued" to everything even if it is not our property, and this helps us live in a world without separations and without abandoned forms of life.

As owners, we are more concerned for the wellbeing

of what we have linked ourselves to than for their material usefulness to us. For example, if mining a mountain that is a special part of our world would damage it or poison the river born from it, then we prefer not to do it, even if this means losing the opportunity to receive large sums of money. Maintaining the unity of our world by not betraying the trust between humans and other life forms that care for and protect each other is a deeper, more lasting kind of wealth. Andean culture is highly relational; the heart connections between humanity and the rest of Nature are the only enduring source of wealth so we value our good relationship with other forms of life as precious above all else. This wealth remains abundant and flowing through respect, tenderness and the consistent practice of feeding each other in a powerful reciprocity.

One of the highest positions an Andean person may be given by their people is to be named "owner of the heart of the territory." The Q'ero people of Cusco regarded my dear elder Martin Paucar in this way, as a *Pampamisayuq*. The word *pampa* refers to a huge flat territory surrounded by mountains, the word *misa* to an altar, and the suffix *yuq* to the owner. So his people considered him to be the owner of the heart, or altar, of a huge territory where the Q'ero people live, love, farm, raise alpacas and talk to the mountains. Holding this position meant he "owned" the people as well. But it didn't mean that Tayta Martin could have sold the land, exploited it for personal benefit, or used the people as servants. In fact, he couldn't even tell the people what to do. By contrast, by owning the land and the people, Tayta Martin was also owned by them, intricately linked to them, responsible for their lives, a humble yet powerful guardian that could be entirely trusted. Tayta Martin was one of the men in charge of preparing the offerings to Pachamama and the Mountain Spirits, so he was trusted as someone who kept the balance of Nature, securing the well-being of the people and their plants, animals and sources of clean water.

During the days of our visit to that jungle of the Sapara people in Ecuador, there was nothing to be afraid of because the owner had given us permission to stay there. I slept so well every night, knowing the jaguar was around protecting us. I felt free to take walks and explore, unafraid of snakes or any other poisonous creatures. Of course I knew I still had to stay centered and help our group remain in the highest vibration possible because the owner can sense all that is going on in its territory. It was important that I remain calm and show respect to every form of life surrounding us, even when simply speaking about them. Powerful owners instinctively empower everything that nourishes what they protect, and, likewise, they leap into action when there is any threat, physical or vibrational, to the health of their territory. Owners deeply feel in their body what is going on in their territory, and they will respond at any moment when their territory falls out of balance. In this way of thinking, feelings are vibrational perceptions different from emotions. A true owner immediately feels the presence of a vibrational frequency antagonistic to the harmonic frequency that keeps its domain alive and healthy. By paying close attention to these sensations, the owners know what they need to know.

Our lack of ownership of our territories allowed entities like the Monsanto Company to claim control over the seeds of our food, the most precious gift our Mother Earth has bestowed upon us. However, Monsanto and any other companies that genetically modify seeds are not solely to blame. Because if someone steals my wallet while I am in a drunken slumber, then I have some responsibility in the loss. In the modern world, the true owners are missing. Most of all, they are missing in people's hearts. The essential wild creature designed to be the owner of a person's body and of all that the person loves was tamed and educated in school, taught good manners, and generally silenced by moral and intellectual social standards that dictate the attributes of an acceptable, well-mannered person. It has become nearly impossible for an individual to claim ownership of what he or she cares for because the real owner, a tender and fierce wild being, a seeming rebel in a world so full of unprotected life, is held captive in a secret place of the mind where it cannot be seen crying or heard screaming. Yet for the Earth to be protected, we need many more people who really own themselves and can eventually own the territory where they live, caring for the well-being of the natural sources of their lives. If the Earth continues to be destroyed, it is because she doesn't have enough real human "owners". Working together, groups of "owners" of various parts of the Earth could make manifest a change that now seems to be impossible. To hold a few unmodified seeds in the palms of our hands and with a prayer decide to be their carriers and caretakers is always a good way to start being "the owners," the same as the Earth People.

CHAPTER NINE

YUYAYKUY

REMEMBER, BE INTELLIGENT

When fully present in our bodies, we have immense capacity to perceive frequencies of vibration that influence the state of living things. If we do not complicate ourselves with excessive head-centered thinking, we naturally know what needs to be done and have the power to do it. We even have tremendous ability to transform the reality. To pick up a rattle and sing a song can change the state of things in seconds. To think with pure tobacco, smoking for just a few minutes, can bring the Earth back into our spirits and then out, renewed, blown through our mouths with the power to improve the state of our world. This can be done anywhere and anytime, under the star-studded sky or within the climate-controlled air of a meeting room.

The ancient practices of our ancestors have become

a necessity and the hunger for that earth-based wisdom among people of all heritages is stronger than ever before. As Albert Einstein said, a problem cannot be solved using the same method that created it. The wise methods of ancient indigenous cultures are re-emerging as an alternative source of effective ways of bringing nature back into balance.

The work of recuperation of our lands and waters will require the highest expression of human intelligence. I find it fascinating that for our ancestors, particularly to the Runasimi speakers, people were considered intelligent when they could remember. In our language we use the word *yuyay* to refer to "intelligence" and "understanding," and it also means "to remember."

But what do we need to remember? Is it the wisdom of our ancestors carried in our genes? Is it the words of wisdom of our elders? Is it the insights received in dreams and ceremonies? All this is important, but nothing can really be remembered if we don't remember ourselves first, meaning our presence in our body in the moment. In Andean culture, we say *"Yuyaykuy"* to remind someone in a tender way to come into fuller presence and fuller intelligence. This word essentially means, "Hey, remember with tenderness!"

I can speak from experience and honestly say that I only feel ready to benefit the Earth with my work when

I remember myself, when I remember to be the owner of my body, when I remember to be one with *my* Earth. So I constantly move my will to return to a completely grounded state of being, centered not in my head but in my earthly core. Much of my work has to do with fiercely protecting life and so I do the best I can to make full use of my body as an instrument that feels, smells, learns and moves in synchronicity with Nature.

In our culture, this grounded state of being that allows us to "own" our territory and care for all that we love is related to the power of the Puma and the Jaguar. Pumas and Jaguars walk long distances in the same middle world where we humans live. They take from the land only what they need, with their eyes and ears wide open, constantly aware of what is going on in their surroundings. People of the Andes who possess this Puma intelligence carry a keen awareness of all that is happening in their territory and kindle a fierce determination to protect it; therefore, they are deeply trusted by their community. The Puma within the human is a wild creature, a natural being, an integral piece of the fabric of Earth, guided by Nature, by the Sun, the Moon and the Stars. It is someone who knows the ways of the Earth and who knows how to live here and now. This intelligence lives in all the natural protectors of vast territories. This intelligence of our heart, the guardian and owner of the territory, knows that the space where all that we love lives begins in our own body. From many oral stories, we know that our ancestors made the utmost use of their body's physical-mental-energetic potential and were capable of doing things that today would be considered supernatural, like moving huge stones or channeling water where it seemed to be impossible. What has been almost forgotten is that they activated not only themselves but also the lands where they lived. Lands were known to be an extension of the human body and there was a partnership between the people and their lands in which they each activated the potential powers of the other. In our time, when we aspire to reverse the crisis in the natural environment that sustains our lives, we could benefit from fully owning our bodies like our ancestors did and working in intimate partnership with our lands.

Pumas and Jaguars have a powerful partner in the underworld: *Amaru*, the sacred snake. When remembering our whole selves, we also remember our snake intelligence, the mind of the Earth that lives in our body, the intelligence that sprouts from our inner underworld. Our body is made of the Earth. The body knows, through its instincts, its perceptual powers and its adaptation abilities, how to find the sources of its health. The snake intelligence of the body is our natural, relational, sexual essence. It doesn't require education, only the proper nourishment and practices. It is spontaneous and can adapt to the constantly changing conditions of the life surrounding us. When our thoughts and emotions learn to trust in the body and do not interfere with this pure bodily knowledge, we move with fluid certainty through all the complexities of life. Aligned with our snake intelligence, we have full trust that our body knows what the Earth knows. To move in the world with this confidence gives a true power to our actions. Because of this, in ours and other cultures the presence of snakes in stone carvings, in pieces of pottery or in textiles refers to the presence of a natural, instinctive wisdom.

Another important aspect of ourselves we remember when in need of our highest intelligence is our Condor side. The Condor is a partner of Pumas and Jaguars that resides in the upper world. While Puma protects all that lives in his territory, Condor loves everything in all territories. Our Condor intelligence makes us remember the well-being of all life everywhere. Condor intelligence is the remembrance that everything is connected and that we can only be really well when all life is well.

The integration of these three intelligences is called *Qoa Chinchay*, a state of being depicted in the Andean image of a snake blending its body with that of a puma, forming a creature with a snake-like middle and a puma's paws and head. This snake-puma flies carried by the condor's power, rising from the shores of a lake toward the forming clouds in the sky, slapping them with its tail to make thunder and rain and gift the land with abundant water. *Qoa Chinchay*, a part-snake, part-puma, condor-flying being is an ancient figure. In this old worldview, we are intelligent when we remember how to "make rain," when we have, in one way or another, the power to nourish the health and continuity of life. This capacity requires full activation of our three intelligences. A seamless integration of body, heart and spirit is necessary because only when all parts of us are acting as a single unit can our actions have total conviction. The picture of *Qoa Chinchay* beating the clouds with its tail makes me feel the power of conviction, a doubtless state of being that makes things happen.

When our thinking head is the only source of our actions, we may have doubts and lack real conviction for having a real influence on the state of our world. Once the head seizes control, the body is forgotten, the heart is dismissed, and our three intelligences do not unify as one. The schools and education centers of the modern world are mainly focused on feeding the head's intelligence; the memory of a powerful way of being human cannot be fully rekindled in them. Only when we are exposed to the energy of those men and women who embody a unification of all three intelligences and have this power alive in them does our desire for it truly appear. When the longing is strong enough, the activation begins. Everything — the Earth, the Universe, the ancient heart of humanity — supports our intention and effort. Among our efforts is participation in ceremonies. We perform ceremonies to remember and to again feel the longing to awaken. In our ceremonies we destroy all assumptions, especially about our own power or capacities, and experience a moment of pure awareness that helps us truly see ourselves. As we become aware of our actual state of being, we often realize that, once more, we need to put back together all of our parts, reassemble ourselves, have the Puma of our heart call in the Snake and call in the Condor, and fly like *Qoa Chinchay*.

CHAPTER TEN

MAÑAKUY

PRAYER

There are two very significant changes to life on Earth unfolding in the present moment. One is an accelerated ascension in the vibrational frequency of life forms; the other, caused by human forgetfulness, is climate change. Many autoimmune illnesses have emerged because the minds and bodies of most people have not been "upgraded" with the natural instructions necessary to adapt to these large-scale, rapid changes.

Human nations have always received the instructions needed for their survival and well-being through growing and eating local foods. When we eat good food and drink clean water, we absorb and digest the light they carry, a cosmic light filled with information that guides the healthful development of life. Our body begins to understand and follow the light's guidance even before our head can register the instructions. Later on, we enjoy the experience of "inspiration" when the instructions stored in our body finally integrate with our thoughts and give us the wisdom to make good decisions and participate with awareness in the real happenings of the Earth.

In the lands of the Andes, many people still have the good fortune to eat food grown on their own farms or on nearby farms. Even if in some areas the diet is not highly varied, with corn and potatoes often being the main food, at least they can eat what grows in their homelands, as healthy Earth People always do, thereby absorbing the knowledge and power of the land where they live. In the cities and many other places in the world, genetically modified or highly processed foods transported in ships and trucks over long distances are now the most accessible. So the light of the Sun, as well as the local land, cannot communicate with the bodies of people through what they eat. In many cities around the world, people's response to this life-threatening reality is to build personal organic gardens and grow at least some of their own food, a beautiful effort that attests to how deeply they value their health.

Another way people are responding to the feeling of being separated from Nature's guidance is through prayer. Despite the limitations imposed by modern life, I have visited many countries where people refuse to become unhealthy and pray regularly as a way to communicate with the Earth and the Universal Sources of Life, often emulating the ways of indigenous peoples. Even though communication with the Earth and the Universe by eating Nature's pure harvest has been so reduced, it is beautiful to witness how humans somehow remember what we have to do despite the obstacles. Instinctively, we always find ways to adapt and grow, discovering a light to guide us through the darkness. In the past, I do not recall seeing so many people gathering stones and other sacred objects to build altars in their homes, or incensing those altars and homes with the smoke of sacred plants, or playing the traditional music of indigenous cultures, or praying out in Nature and opening a line of communication with the Sacred Powers.

For indigenous people, prayer has always been a simple and powerful form of communication. Prayer is about cultivating relationships; it is a way of speaking and listening that helps us to relate well with someone or something sacred. The purpose of our ceremonies is to receive help, to offer help, or to express our gratitude for help we have received. Speaking, singing or dancing with the sacred owners of natural spaces, with the spirits of the animals, with the spirits of the plants, with the spirit of water, we eventually come near to the very source of all vitality, the feeder of all spirits and all life, a generous sacred energy in permanent motion that is ever powerful, and respectfully communicate directly with it.

In my experience, prayer is a state of being more than an articulation of words. The state of our being when praying in ceremony allows for communication with Spirit. For me, to pray is to completely open my mind, my heart and my body so something sacred may enter me or come out of me. I intend to become liberated from the controls of my human mind and totally open to being overtaken by Spirit. If there are any words, they are the direct result of being in this state of intimate connection to the heart of life. Strong and sincere, these words fly with enormous force, like arrows shot cleanly at a star. Swiftly, they arrive to their destination: an open wound in the heart of the Sacred, a wound created by our forgetfulness. When our words tenderly touch the wound we caused in her when we left and forgot that she is our Mother, she remembers us and begins to pull us back to her center. What a blissful feeling to be swept into the magnetic field of the Universal Mother's womb! Yet, we soon forget her again, and so we pray again, and we forget and we pray again, and again, and again.

I have been praying all my life. I am grateful to my elders for showing me how they do it because it truly works. By communicating through prayer, I am more likely to remain healthy, ever nourished by the sacred source of vitality. Through many years working as a healer, I have discovered what many others also know: that severe illnesses may originate from losing communication with the sources of vitality, forgetting to ask for what we need or to give thanks for all we are given. An Apache medicine man I once knew used to talk to the water in his glass before beginning to drink. He explained to me that everything has a spirit and everything is medicine, so we need to remember to ask the spirits for what we need. He said he was healthy because he always asked the water to clear any problems that may be happening in his body.

Recently, I walked past the bathroom in my home and heard my three-year-old daughter talking to someone. I stopped so I could hear better what was going on, and realized that she was by herself, brushing her teeth. She was talking to her teeth. She was asking them to never break or have holes and promising them, in the most tender tone of voice, that she would always take good care of them. I am sure if she keeps talking to her teeth in that way she will never have to go to a dentist!

In one way or another, illness often has to do with a lack of communication that results in a lack of nourishment and a poor circulation of energy. The same energy that circulates in outer space enters our planet and becomes earthly energy, and this earthly energy needs to enter our body and become ours. Once in our body, it can reach all our parts, large and tiny, and give them the vitality and instructions they need. Through sincere and skillful communication, we humans can direct these movements of energy and take care of our health.

In the modern world, the excessive use of smart phones is the clearest manifestation of an atrophy occurring in people's communication skills. To observe people using communication devices to isolate themselves is like watching someone eat to become hungry. It doesn't make any sense. Good communication is the key to maintaining our connection to Nature, belonging to everything, exposing ourselves to receive the energy that circulates everywhere and later on become givers of energy ourselves. When I see people so separated from Nature and from other people, seeking intimacy through their devices with those that are far away and avoiding the vulnerability of close contacts, I pray that one day their divine spark will ignite and give them the courage to be less fearful and dare to expose themselves. From my experience of working with people in ceremony, I know that unless someone who is closed and blocked kindles the will to be in open communication with the Earth, the Spirit World and their human friends, they may eventually contract a serious illness. Ironically, illness, working as a strong wake up call, is sometimes the only cure for people who are unaware of the isolated state in which they have put themselves.

No one is free from the possibility of illness, yet we all have a greater chance of maintaining our health by avoiding all the feeble nourishment our forgetful modern society propagates and all the ways modern technology limits our experience of the true and deep communication we need. At the very least, we could make sure our body stays aligned with the growth of the Earth and that we do not deprive ourselves of the wisest plants, waters and air by consuming unnatural, man-made products that interrupt the communication between the Earth and our bodies, between the Sun and our bodies, and between all the parts of our bodies.

The cultures of Earth People are based on making and caring for relationships, and relationships depend upon good communication. Our capacity to connect with others is so important that we do not give it over to something external such as a technological device. Rather we take personal ownership of our communicative powers and develop them in the rich environment of a communitarian life where learning to listen well and to express what we carry inside begins in childhood and continues throughout our life. We don't have to wait for new technology to upgrade our capacity to communicate; we upgrade ourselves through leading lives of constant growth, opening ourselves more and more and defending ourselves less and less. This personal growth is revealed in an increased capacity to touch the tender being of another, and become good medicine to those that are suffering from lack of communication.

In many indigenous cultures someone is considered an elder, a person of wisdom, when they demonstrate an elevated ability to communicate deeply with other people, with Nature, and with the spirit world. These are the ones who can say much with very few words, who sometimes don't need words at all to communicate something so precious that it becomes nourishment and medicine for all those around them. Our elders help us remember to continually refine our communication with the sacred powers, for it is this communication that feeds the health and happiness of all life. The fact that human suffering releases energy which can then feed the Earth's plasma might make it seem that the world is cruelly indifferent. But the truth is we are constantly given the opportunity to grow our consciousness and nourish all that lives through the energy of powerful prayer rather than through great suffering. The spirit world, the divine light, and the sacred energy in permanent motion always invite us to learn and develop, and our spiritual formation has much to do with learning to be in good communication with these sacred powers.

PART TWO:
THUNDER

Not necessarily in a gentle manner,
Thunder and Lightning strike,
shaking all life, awakening the dormant.
Born in the West,
where the blue light shines before the dark night,
this immense thunderstorm love doesn't expect to be liked
or loved back. It changes what needs to change.
It releases water onto our lands at will
and helps us to be powerfully small.

CHAPTER ELEVEN

PUKLLAY

To Play

A sign on the wall of a good restaurant in the little town of Pisaq near the city of Cusco in Peru reads: "We make magic, but we don't make miracles." This little quip feels true in regard to the efforts that many people and organizations are making on behalf of the Earth. Will the waters of Mother Earth suddenly be healed by a miracle? Probably not, but surely magicians can be involved in the necessary work, people who practice the art of deep observation and can communicate with the Earth and the Universe and attract lots of assistance to bring about the best possible future.

In the Andes where I come from, five hundred years have passed since the Spanish invasion and now we are suffering the new invasion of a high-tech, globalized, commercial culture and its devastating impact upon our lands and water sources. Just as the white layer of ice and snow that for thousands of years capped the peaks of our mountains is suddenly turning gray, everything is changing way too fast.

Above all else, our ancestors most deeply loved the waters of the Earth, so deeply they dedicated temples to them, sacred places in which they carefully built channels to observe and follow the movements that water knows how to do. In these temples, the sacred power of the water was honored as the singing messenger of the sources of life, as the most able purifier of the human soul, as the highest revitalizing nourishment, and as the mirror, the flow, and the one that gives life to all the other medicines needed for life. Today, while still surrounded by our ancestral temples dedicated to water, we drink from plastic bottles and have come to believe the power to heal our environment is in the hands of those who control the technology that created the damage in the first place. Our indigenous people, who have eaten organic foods for thousands of years and given the natural remainders back to the Earth are now, without really realizing it, polluting their home environment by throwing plastic containers in the land and rivers as if they were banana peels. On the other hand, most of our traditional people help to heal the environment just by being the way they are.

In Pisaq, as in most Andean towns, people pray to

water during the entire month of February to give thanks for the flowering of their crops and of the world. This celebration was given the name Carnival by the European invaders who had similar observances in their cultures, but the original Runasimi name is *Pukllay*, which means "to play." And people really play during that time, especially with water! You must be careful when walking the streets in February or else be ready to play, because the youth will splash you with water and laugh like crazy. Nobody gets mad at those who throw water at them. We just laugh even if we have to go back home and change clothes, just to come out and get wet again.

The highlight of *Pukllay* in Pisaq are the dances that happen one Sunday in February. Groups of musicians and dancers arrive from numerous indigenous communities. They all take a turn presenting their dance of the year, each more powerful and beautiful than the other. Because it is *Pukllay*, the dances can be sensual and involve lots of play between men and women who will pull and push each other flirtatiously. It is so beautiful to watch! And it is no coincidence that the main Catholic holiday dedicated to bless newborns in the Cusco area happens about nine months after *Pukllay*!

Last year, my friend Isidro and his wife Vicky decided to revive the celebration of *Pukllay* in their community of Cotataki, and they honored my wife and me by asking for our help and participation. The aim was to do it as it was done in the old days when it was a pure Andean ceremony of fertility and gratitude. With the support of Isidro's father, who is the mayor of the Cotataki community, the ceremony was celebrated there for the first time in twelve years. The youth are typically the main participants in *Pukllay*; but because of the influence of modern life or the need to take jobs away from home, most of the young people of Cotataki were largely missing from the ceremony. They were really surprised when Isidro sent videos and pictures of our *Pukllay*. Initially, they thought the images were records from ceremonies held long ago, but when they learned the ceremony had been revived, all those who had left home vowed to come back and participate the following year.

First, we climbed to the peak of the mountain *Wayraqpunku*, or "the door of the winds," and stopped for a moment to pray to Pachamama and the *Apukuna* to express our gratitude. We then descended on the other side of the mountain to the site where the community of Cotataki has celebrated *Pukllay* since ancient times, an area flat enough for people to dance. There we chewed coca leaves, drank chicha, ate capuli fruits and shared our abundance with the mountain. Isidro took the opportunity to tell all those present about the last time he witnessed the ceremony when he was still a little boy. He saw the young men come to the same mountain where we were and spend hours collecting panti flowers to give to the girls as adornments for their hats and to carry as medicine for colds. Meanwhile the girls, somewhere on the same mountain, looked for capuli fruits to share with the boys before the dance.

In his story, Isidro highlighted the moment at sunset when the girls, seemingly looking for capuli with innocence, bumped into precisely the boy they liked somewhere in one of the natural shelters made by big rocks and shady trees. And how, as it was too late to find the way back home, they had to spend the night together in the arms of their sacred mountain and of each other for lack of a blanket. Many of my female friends in Cusco have told me with a big smile on their face that their children are blessed because they were conceived during *Pukllay*! The ceremony always coincides with the harvest of corn and the arrival of the most intense rains. This is the time when the land is greenest, when the frogs sing the most, and when most creatures are busy making babies and building nests. It is a time to celebrate sexuality as the power of Nature and honor love as a commitment to be tender to and grateful for one another every step of the way.

As soon as Isidro finished his story, the musicians began to play and the girls each invited a boy to dance with them. That beautiful moment ignited a spirit of pure joy in all of us, and we became like colorful wildflowers dancing in the mountain wind. After the abundant exchange of coca leaves, chicha, and capuli, as well as all the sensual dancing, the men felt well nourished by the women and the women by the men, and the mountain by their mutual happiness! The return home was an ordered ritual in which all who went to the mountain separately came back together, forming the most beautiful line of couples dancing their way down, followed by the musicians in the back, and me behind them all since my wife and our baby were waiting for me down below. All of us were blissfully happy, swimming in the joyful spill of the waterfall we had become.

Another time, a few days before the dances of *Pukllay* in Pisaq, I was observing a mountain named *Phaqchayuq*, which means "the one that has the waterfall," and felt sad because there was no waterfall that year. Immediately after the celebration of *Pukllay*, it began to rain heavily and the rains continued for days and days as they are supposed to in February. There was so much rain that one day, to my surprise, I saw the waterfall had returned full of life. I prayed in gratitude:

> *Thank you, Pachamama; thank you, Thunder Beings; thank you, children for playing so joyfully with the water; thank you, dancers and musicians; thank you, lovers who freed your sexuality and became pregnant;*

*thank you, singing frogs and flowers and all of you
who call forth more life so we may all continue to be
here, in this wonderful space, at this wonderful time!*

CHAPTER TWELVE

YANANTIN

THE COMPLIMENT OF TWO
THAT ARE DIFFERENT

The forces of life continually compose an arrangement of contradictions that our reasoning helps us cope with as best it can. Without the heart, our rational mind cannot easily digest contradictions and tries to resolve them by simply eliminating one of the two parts in conflict. The modern mind tends to get stuck in the rigid structure of two choices, right and wrong, having to stop constantly in order to decide what to accept and what to reject, unable to keep a flow like water moving around and through rocks in a river. But when combined with the heart, our reasoning embraces all aspects of a reality, becoming capable of articulating and expressing what is being observed without taking sides, and thus it flows like all healthy energies do.

Ancient people understood the importance of having an inclusive mind and trained themselves to combine feminine and masculine ways of interpreting reality, which allowed them to follow their heads and their hearts simultaneously. Like any other common man, for many years I used reason to eliminate contradictions, to protect others and myself from the unpredictable wildness of our world, from how dangerous it felt that much of reality seemed different from how I was or how I believed the world should be. But through a life of ceremony my eyes have been washed into a deeper vision, and I can now practice a way of reasoning that does not take sides but instead allows two opposites to dance together until the face of a third presence starts showing up. Today I engage my heart to feel into what wants to be born from the union of the opposites and stand at its service, like a midwife, ready to catch and hold the future with respect. This is important to me because where something wants to be born, there is water, there is life, and I am training my eyes to find water everywhere, refusing to live in a dry world.

In this moment, the Earth is in danger because of the destruction of Nature caused by human activity. Our ability to respond to the crisis without delay is often blocked by all the rational, "black or white" considerations we make before acting. Many people only follow their linear masculine intelligence and when that intelligence is uncertain about where a course of action will lead, they simply don't act and remain stagnant. To accept both, black *and* white, and continue flowing behind the power of a strong impulse of the heart's feminine intelligence feels too risky. So the extinction of life on Earth continues to happen in plain view of the most resourceful people.

To prevent the stagnation caused by our mental rigidity, indigenous cultures created complex ceremonial ways of making two opposites play together and complement each other, opposites such as masculine and feminine, above and below, ancient and new, dark and luminous, gentle and fierce. In Runasimi, the complement of two that are different and opposite is called *Yanantin* — while for the complement of two that are similar we use the word *Masintin*. The *Yanantin* principle is one of the pillars of the Andean mind. Without its inclusive power, our Andean and Amazonian people wouldn't have made it through the brutality of the conquest and colonization. Our culture is always guided by this principle, as can be clearly seen in our dances that have the power to call rain and bring new life. One is named *Machu Tusuy* and is the dance of the Elders, a beautiful ceremony performed every year in the Cusco area where the dancers dress like very old rugged-looking men and move supported by crooked staffs. The power of this ceremony lies in its activation of *Yanantin*, for young boys are disguised as old men and one young man, the strongest and most vital dancer in the group, is dressed as a woman.

I once saw the young man dressed as a woman pull an old man passing by who could hardly walk into the dance circle and make him dance! It was amazing to witness how the old man began to loosen up; invigorated with a new energy, suddenly he was moving like a young man!

At the climax of the *Machu Tusuy* dance, the "old men" let go of their staffs and begin to dance much more vigorously, impressing the crowd. The costumed old men embody the fruits of humanity, which hold the seeds of our future within them, and the children inside the costumes are the future itself, the fertile ground where the seeds will fall and germinate. In putting together the old and the new, life is restored and renewed. The sacred union of opposites embodied by the youth dressed as elders and the man dressed as a woman gives the ceremony its power; it calls in the forces that continue to generate life.

In Arequipa, where I was born, there is the deepest canyon in the world, Collca Canyon, a place also with the largest population of huge condors. For the ancient indigenous people of this region, Collca Canyon was a sacred site where powerful observations were made, in part because the lowest entity, the canyon floor, and the highest, the soaring condor, inhabit that space together. It is also well known that some condors from Collca Canyon travel hundreds of miles every day from the Andes Mountains to the ocean and a place called Paracas, the site of an ancient pre-Inca culture. These condors, in their long daily flight searching for food for their chicks, continually connect the lowest and the highest and thereby create a movement and circulation of energy that our ancestors knew to be sacred. To this day, when we prepare offerings high up in the Andes and ask for healing, for rain and for the well-being of all life, there must be elements from the ocean down below included in the bundle, at least a shell and a starfish. And when we make offerings on the seashore, there must be stones or medicine plants from high up in the mountains included in it. Again, the union of these opposites, above and below, gives power to the offering. When we connect the mountaintop and the ocean, we follow the Sun's example when he makes rain by evaporating water from the ocean and bringing it up to the mountains in the form of dark clouds. The condor is a student of the Sun, and we are students of both the condor and the Sun.

The two major indigenous groups that live in Collca Canyon, the Cabanas and the Collawas, also form a polarity. In the old days, the Cabanas used skull deformation techniques to elongate their heads to make them look like mountains while the Collawas flattened theirs to make them look almost square, like the plateau. Even today, these two nations living side by side in the Collca Canyon dress differently in order to retain the charge of that polarity. The name Cabana is a Spanish version of the Runamsimi word *qhawana* meaning "observatory." The *Qhawana Runa* were "the people of vision" and their territory was a place where observations were made. Like the condor, their ancestors were adept at seeing the big picture in life, looking in all directions and through all times.

The name Collawa comes from the word *colla* that refers to the highest lands of Altiplano around Lake Titiqaqa. The Collawa were people who decided to change their environment and live in a lower place when they migrated from the very cold Altiplano to the warmer Collca Canyon. They then became specialized in things of below, mastering knowledge of the abundant medicines and material resources of the new land around them. This teaches us not everyone has to develop high spiritual vision and, likewise, not everyone has to tend to all the material needs of life. We always need both kinds of people, and only a few people carry both talents skillfully. Similarly, a woman doesn't have to be a man, and a man doesn't have to be a woman. Not everyone has to be vessels of water and not everyone has to be conduits of fire and only a few are good channels for both. The principle of polarity requires that the two ends of every power that bring life remain diametrically opposed so that when they unify, life is generated. This is why men and women are required to dress differently from one another in our ceremonies.

For the Lakota People of North America, the principle of polarity exists in the most sacred instrument used for prayer, the *Cannunpa* or sacred pipe. The *Cannunpa* has two parts, the bowl made out of pipestone that holds the herb called *cincasa* and receives the fire when smoked and the stem made from wood which sends the smoke into our mouths. Every Lakota ceremony, from the simplest to the most elaborate, begins at the moment the stem and the bowl of the *Cannunpa* are connected and it ends when they are separated. This is just like the lovemaking that can conceive a child and bring new life. When the stem penetrates the bowl, the magic begins, the two have become one, the sacred has been activated, and life is being generated once again. In that sacred moment, the reality within and around us is immediately elevated to a higher frequency where possibilities beyond the ordinary are present and our capacity to hear deeply, to heal, to understand and to forgive is enhanced. In this state, our minds open to wiser levels of reasoning that we express as prayer.

The *Canunnpa* is a sort of temple that my Lakota relatives and all those who carry it in a good way can bring anywhere, a temple that is rebuilt over and again by connecting the bowl, the feminine, and the stem, the masculine. Temples are what we build to bring our presence in front of the presence of the Sacred. The bringing of masculine and feminine together is always essential when building a temple, like in Chavin, one of the most important sacred sites in the Andes. This temple, originally named Chawpin, is very dear to me because I spent a great deal of time there in my twenties, exposing myself as much as possible to its vibration and carefully observing all that was around me while asking the ancestors to lift me into a state of greater understanding. Chawpin, meaning the place of the middle, was built thousands of years ago by extremely wise people. At this sacred site, archeologists have not been able to find the typical stages of evolution or archeological levels that demonstrate the progress a human culture makes over long periods of time as they refine their technology and use of materials. The people of Chawpin knew what they were doing the first time they did it and created a jewel of architecture that although affected by earthquakes and mudslides throughout the centuries is still standing in its great beauty and power.

There are so many fascinating elements in the way

Chawpin was designed. One is that just in front of the temple's main stone structure (which originally had four levels underground and three levels above ground), there is something like a big square plaza. There is evidence that it was once filled with water and served as some sort of pool or water altar. If you stand right on the edge of the pool, facing the temple so the pool is between you and the temple, there will be two steps below you. On the first, a little circle is carved on the vertical side facing the temple. If a line is projected from this circle right through the pool, it arrives at exactly the point where the temple is divided into two halves, one side made of dark stones and the other made of light, almost white-colored stones. Moreover, the wall on the right side of the temple is completely vertical while the wall on the left side is at an eight degree incline. All of this is *Yanantin,* the complement of opposites. *Yanantin* was clearly a very important spiritual principle for the ancient sages who built Chawpin in such a precise way and with enormous effort.

In the Cusco region, near Paucartambo, there is a beautiful little Inca temple named Watoqto that sits on a hill. Looking down from the temple, one can see that at the bottom of the hill two rivers intersect. Our ancestors always chose points of sacred geography to place their sacred architecture. In this case, they chose the intersection of two rivers, which means this temple was dedicated to the power of *Yanantin*. Chawpin was also built at the intersection of two rivers.

My wife, Marilyn, and I once traveled to Watoqto with our Q'ero elder Martin Paucar. Tayta Martin had told us many months before that he would be giving us a *Misa*, an altar for us to use in ceremony. He said that this would be a *Yanantin* altar to be used to pray with the energy of the union of opposites. I had seen *Yanantin* temples, *Yanantin* stone altars in temples, and *Yanantin* ceremonial instruments throughout my life, but I had never seen a *Yanantin* altar carried by a ceremonial leader to use for prayer. In the many months after Tayta Martin told Marilyn and me that he wanted to give us this altar, I kept wondering what it was, how it looked, what elements and spirits it contained. When the ceremony started and Tayta Martin displayed all the items he would use to make the *haywarikuy,* the offering to the *Apukuna* mountain spirits, there were two altars present, one for me and one for Marilyn. To my surprise and delight, they were the most simple altars I had ever seen, woven mantas made by Mama Martina, Tayta Martin's wife, each with a line in the middle dividing two sides, one light-colored and the other dark-colored. That was it, a *Yanantin* altar designed much like the temple of Chawpin.

Receiving an altar always involves some type of initiation, and it isn't always an easy one. An altar is only real when it comes from the spirit world. This means the Sacred Spirits are really the ones who give it to someone using a human spiritual leader as their instrument. There are often tests to pass and limitations to overcome that prove you are strong enough to carry the altar without being crushed by its power. Marilyn and I barely made it. The night before the ceremony, we began having terrible communication with each other and huge misunderstandings. She felt I wasn't recognizing something in her heart that she couldn't express in words, and I felt rejected by her refusal to follow what I thought was a good direction for us in that moment - a normal scenario for couples but very difficult because it happened just before the ceremony. When we met Tayta Martin the next morning to travel to Watoqto, he was surprised by our bad mood. I had much to learn that day watching him move forward with the ceremony like a determined puma, following through with what he said he would do even though he saw there were mixed feelings between Marilyn and me.

We each received our *Yanantin* altars in that state of fear of being left by the other, in a state of doubt about our ability to stay together. I now see how perfect that was. Receiving an altar in indigenous culture is far from a prize or a celebration of your talents. Rather it is a responsibility, a sacred bundle to be carried for the well-being of all life, a healing instrument, a balancing force.

So as we received the altar we had to see our true capacity and its limits and decide if we were really able to live with the power of *Yanantin* in our lives. Truthfully, we are still working on it. What our elder really gave us was the opportunity to do the work of holding the polarity without any escape. The deep love we have for each other allows us to walk this intense path together. We must grow up and, as we do, we continue praying to become a good example to young couples that want to learn about the healthy relationship of masculine and feminine, of fire and water. We know we are not there yet, just as humanity is not there yet. However, we deeply want to get there and we are trying, just as humanity is trying. The journey of constantly putting two opposites together is easy and difficult, at times so bright and at times so dark.

The super lightweight *Yanatin* altar is in many ways the heaviest I have ever received. Marilyn and I are both recovering from having parents who are separated and from growing up in a world where all the main complementary forces have been split apart. Over time, this sacred bundle has become lighter, or perhaps we are growing stronger together as well as becoming softer, especially in walking with a precious little one who is the beautiful sweet fruit of our union. In the Andean world, as my brother Bacilio says, one plus one is three. Our dear Tayta Martin called our daughter *Munay Tika*,

Flower of the Heart. This reminds me that despite our limitations and shortcomings we are doing well. In our opposite natures my wife and I have given life to a Flower of the Heart, a flower that someday will have her own little fruits, girls and boys who will live in a new culture on the Earth, one in which the partnership of men and women powerfully generates and sustains life, where the male fire does not dry out the female water and where feminine water doesn't drown out the masculine fire.

CHAPTER THIRTEEN

SUPAYCHA

LITTLE DEVIL

From the indigenous perspective, no healing can happen without inclusiveness, without putting things together so they can maintain constant communication and form a good relationship in the end. Some energies are what we call a good match and they form a partnership easily; others are so opposite it seems their destiny is to constantly fight each other. But the truth is when generating life there is nothing more powerful than making opposites be complementary. I have traveled to places like the Middle East where hate and fear have grown between nations. As an outsider, I can easily see what many of them can't. There is enormous opportunity for the next generations of their countries if they become partners instead of enemies. Who says we cannot love those with whom we are in conflict? If they were to maintain a more peaceable conflict, it would serve to keep both sides awake and to mature together through their mutual struggle. But when one seeks the elimination of the other, an unnatural element takes over, a hatred born of human ego, and no more fruits bloom from the union of two that are different. The only result is unnecessary suffering and death.

In modern times, humanity has been greatly weakened by the obsession with taking sides. The possible union of opposites that could be complementary in their differences is constantly blocked. For many people, it is a cultural habit that begins in childhood to choose one group and reject another, linking their identity to this choice. There are so many opposites we have a hard time putting together. If we were more capable of pairing them, we would have more real power as a society when the time comes to make important changes in our reality.

Ancient peoples were wise and the indigenous values and rituals that exist to this day remind us of the significant role of the contrary. In Lakota culture, for example, there is the *Heyoka* principle. People who incarnate this principle are also called *Heyoka,* and their participation in ceremonies powerfully puts opposites together, like the collision of clouds that makes thunder and rain to create a potent medicine for those ready to end their sickness. The *Heyoka* is a contrary figure, a clown, someone who moves backwards when everyone else moves forward, someone who says, "I hate you" to tell you, "I love you."

At the Lakota Sun Dance, there is always a *Heyoka* present for some part of the four-day ceremony. One of the most powerful moments of the dance comes on the third day when the dancers' bodies are in a weakened state after fasting from food and water and dancing for days. The ceremony is usually held in the middle of summer when it is extremely hot, so by the third day the Sundancers hardly have enough water in their body to make sweat. That is just when the *Heyoka* will suddenly enter the circle with a bowl full of watermelon slices and start eating them right in the dancers' faces, spilling juice all over the ground, laughing and moaning with pleasure. Sometimes he even brings a slice of watermelon very close to a dancer's mouth, tempting him to break his vow to fast during the ceremony, and the dancer has to concentrate on his prayer more than ever.

Some people outside the dance circle supporting the ceremony may find this to be cruel, but I know from experience that the *Heyoka's* actions make you stronger. In truth, they force you to pull out a strength you didn't realize you had stored somewhere deep inside your body. It is amazing how after their clowning, regardless of how exhausted you began the third day of the dance, you somehow end it with more vitality and more happiness than you had on the first day.

Something similar happens in the family home. Life at home is sometimes like a strong ceremony. I am lucky to have a really good *"Heyoka"* to help me, and that is my wife! She is my contrary and is the best helper in my life. When she does her best to make me lose my center, I need to avoid blaming her. If I do that, I will for certain go off-kilter. The only one responsible for holding my center is myself. From her beautifully wild feminine nature, my wife offers me some "watermelon" many times a day, and the more I stay connected to my core, the stronger my core becomes.

Maybe this is what the Hebrew people meant when they spoke about Eve offering Adam the apple from the forbidden tree. The Hebrews had apples and the Lakota have watermelons! Eve was most likely just following her feminine nature and thereby helping Adam become stronger. From an indigenous point of view, repressing Eve and punishing her for being who she is makes men weak while respecting her nature makes the men strong. In this story, there is also the snake. Growing up in a country where Catholic and indigenous cultures live together, I have always felt uncomfortable with the bad reputation given to both women and snakes as evil. I have a mother, I have four daughters, I have a beautiful wife, and I have many snake friends! There are rattlesnakes where I live in New Mexico, and they are the kindest and most beautiful creatures on our land.

They provide an enormous service to us because, thanks to them, we can never be distracted when we walk. We keep our eyes open as we walk and, with this enhanced attention, we don't just see the snakes we don't want to step on, we see other wonderful presences in the land that are our teachers. In the Bible, snakes are seen as female because men authored its books. If women had written those stories, then the snakes would probably be male. For women, men are the contrary.

In original Andean culture, there was actually no notion of good and evil. There is no Runasimi word that literally means bad or evil. The closest thing is to say, "*Mana allin,*" which means "not good." This must have been hard for the Catholic priests who arrived to the Andes with a tradition rooted in saints and devils that never reconcile. They must have had a difficult time trying to make our ancestors understand concepts like hell and punishment from God. It took a long time for the priests to find a word in our language to use in naming the devil. They chose the word *Supay*. In our culture *Supay* originally was and still is an adjective used to acknowledge someone's greatness due to an enormous dedication in some specific discipline. A great soccer player, highly developed in the art and techniques of the sport, can be called, in a mix of Runasimi and Spanish, a "*supay futbolista.*" *Supay* doesn't mean evil but super, as in Superman! And today, after five hundred years of colonization, it also means devil. In Andean ceremonies, our version of the Lakota *Heyoka* is in many places playfully called *Supaycha* or little devil. Even after the Catholics tried to separate the devils from the saints, our people found a way to put them back together, creating this funny little devil character that incarnates the dark side of reality in our sacred ceremonies while also making people laugh.

The Catholic authorities that started using the word *Supay* to name the devil were in a sense very clever. They knew our ancestors perceived those who aspired to personal greatness as potentially dangerous. Not all those who are *Supay* do harm; but if those with powerful influence in a community do not use their gifts to protect the people but instead take vitality from them and from the Earth to feed their individual power only, it can greatly hurt everyone and everything around them. In Andean culture, though, when someone is identified as possibly destructive due to their narcissism, the response is not to call them evil and eliminate them but to leave them be for a while. Accepting their challenging presence, the community learns something and becomes stronger. Often we are ultimately grateful for the mirror they embody so we may see our dark side. They are stopped only when they go too far. In the time of the Inca, someone with an exaggerated *Supaycha* energy was asked to leave the community for a year or so to experience loneliness and lack of help from others.

In our ancient culture, we do not rush to eliminate the devils and accept only the angels because life is made of both. Eliminating the opponent just ends the game, and life is produced by the game, by the movement of natural energy produced by the encounter of opposites. The *Yanantin* altar always has two sides, one light and one dark, and thus it is possible to put something not good on one side and something good on the other. Honoring the service they both provide, we work from the line in the middle, allowing the union of these opposite forces to produce vitality and wisdom useful for the growth and balance of all life. The precious line in the middle disappears when the opposites are split apart or when they are made equal and their differences can no longer be seen.

To have an aversion toward something is seen as a sign of self-importance, so in a culture that requires humility in order to function well, liking or disliking something is out of place. This was so fixed in the mentality of our ancestors that we don't even have a way to say, "I like it" in our language. The verb "to like" wasn't known until our ancestors learned to speak Spanish. So you also cannot say, "I don't like it." That's so good! Imagine a world where kids never say, "I don't like that!" Humbler teenagers mean less headaches for the parents! Things become really difficult at the home when youth seek to build their identity based on what they like and don't like. As if to say, "I don't like peanut butter" defines who they are in some significant way. The danger with emphasizing liking and disliking is that it can lead to saying, "I don't like people of color" or "I hate it when it rains", falling out of the natural order of things to defend an illusory identity built from a lack of contact with one's true essence. To acknowledge when something was good for them or not, the old people said, "I want it" or "I don't want it" and thus avoided building identities based on likes and dislikes. For example, "*Kay mikhunata munani*" means "I want this food" because, in Runasimi, there is no way to say, "I like this food." There is much strength in a culture driven by "wanting" instead of "liking" because in real wanting there is a heart.

Another example is that from the perspective of my Spanish-speaking mind, I may have never written books. I may have been tempted to decide I really don't like to write more than just a few words, that my preference is to play a rattle and put things together with the spirits through the pure vibration of a song. Writing is very hard work, so I would be more drawn to what I can do better, which is shake my rattle in the darkness of a sweatlodge. It is the will born of my Andean heart that inspires me to do not what I like but what my heart deeply wants, which is to serve Pachamama and allow her to move my heart. The will of my heart holds my intentions, not my likes and dislikes, and I own the intention of sharing ancient teachings through writing. After all, I learn so much by doing what is not easy for me. I am forced to think in order to write, and in order to think I have to listen, and listening gives me the honor of being in relationship with she who guides me.

This is a time when we need to fight for life. But it is clear that she isn't guiding me to fight against something or someone. She is asking me to be grateful for what the adversaries help me activate within myself, so I can have a real power to feed life. She wants me to activate wisdom beyond the mentality that makes me right and someone else wrong. I know the Mother of all Life is asking me to disengage from the painful dramas of the world and seek a higher power, difficult for a humble human like me to find, that can put all that exists, shadow and light, together inside an egg of light. So, if I chose to be a warrior, I cannot be angry. I cannot take sides and say I dislike certain political leaders or corporations or capitalism or governments or cars and airplanes. I have it all inside. I have to reconcile the contrary forces within myself. All that is ready to be reconciled and dance together have always lived inside of us. Important changes are ready to happen and they will be real only if we take responsibility for making them happen within ourselves.

CHAPTER FOURTEEN

UNU NINA TUSUY

DANCE OF WATER AND FIRE

While investigating how we could work with the Earth for the healing of her waters, I often asked for help, praying for a dream at night. Some nights, my prayer was answered. I once dreamt I was peeing blood, so much blood that I was filling up a plastic tub, like one you might use to give a bath to a baby. I woke up startled after the dream and ran to the bathroom to pee. When I saw my pee wasn't red, I was so relieved and went back to bed. In the morning at breakfast, I told my wife Marilyn about my dream, describing to her the huge amount of blood that came out of me. Her immediate response was, "Oh, that's good, you finally got your moon time!" We laughed a bit until our baby needed something and we couldn't talk more about it. Four days after, for some reason I had the impulse to turn over the mattress I was sleeping on when I had the dream. To my surprise, there was water under it, very clean, fresh, cold water that the mattress had mysteriously released onto the floor. I immediately associated it with my dream — first blood, then clean water. I knew it was connected to something I had been trying to learn about the healing of the Earth's waters.

Days passed and I still couldn't interpret all of this, so I consulted the owner of water at our home, my wife Marilyn. Her interpretation was so quick and so accurate that it blew my mind and made me wonder why I didn't ask her earlier. She said menstruation is the way women purify their waters and that men also need to purify their waters for the planet to be healthy again. She felt that my dream was a sort of menstruation experience. And she added that, on her moon time, she has almost no control over what happens to her. The forces that are purifying her waters basically take over her body and mind so that at moments her emotions are all over the place and she can do nothing about it. As Marilyn spoke, I tried to imagine, as a man, a state of not being able to control anything that happened to me. That is just the thing, my wife insisted, men have no experience with accepting situations where they are not in charge or in control. At least, we can be thankful for the sweatlodge ceremony that the wise Lakota ancestors gave us so we may sit humbly in front of the hot steam that comes out of red-hot lava rocks and purify our waters by sweating. We can be thankful as well for all the help we receive from our female allies when we become open to listen to them.

Because of industrial human activities run only by masculine minds, the waters of the Earth are no longer as they used to be in the past. During my travels around the world serving Pachamama, I only had the opportunity to drink water directly from a river two times — once in the south of Brazil and the other in the Argentinean Patagonia. In every other wilderness location, people advised me to drink only water in plastic bottles. Less than a hundred years ago, people took all their drinking water directly from springs, rivers and streams. Now the few best sources of clean water are mostly controlled by the kind of owners who are not true protectors of life.

A woman named Maria from a community in the Cusco area told me, "When I was little, everyone in our community drank water directly from springs. The water was delicious and we were all healthy. Now the water sources in the mountains are under private ownership or get treated by the government. What is this treatment? As I see it, they are poisoning our water with chemicals that it didn't have before so I don't want to drink it. My mother always tells me things have changed too much. She is very worried for her grandchildren because there is less and less clean water, and the water we do have is not as good as it used to be. Modernity has screwed us up." Maria's mom, like so many of us, wants to see the illness in our environment come to an end and water to be returned to its natural state so her grandchildren may have a healthy life. Given that illness is often related to lack of good communication, some gifted individuals are going to have to speak to the spirit of Water in order to repair the health of our environment.

An old Quechuan story tells us about a rancher whose property depended on the water of a very productive spring. One day the spring suddenly had much less water flowing from it. The rancher became angry and yelled at the spring, demanding it produce more. Immediately the spring went completely dry. The indigenous farmers who were servants of the rancher depended on the same spring for their sustenance. They knew that when the rancher yelled at the spring, the Spirit of *Yaku*, of Water, left and went far away. So they begged a medicine woman who could talk to Sacred Spirits to intervene for them and ask the Spirit of *Yaku* to return. The old woman happened to know the exact offerings, prayers and songs that the Spirit of Water responds to, and after some effort she was able to call it back to the spring. The people were happy to have water again and the rancher learned never to yell at a spirit again.

This simple story gives us clues about who has the power to bring the water back. Just as the people begged the old woman for her assistance, we need to implore the owners of the Earth's waters to call back the spirit of *Yaku*. These owners are not so far away. We see their presence in the eyes of every little girl, woman and grandmother. The current environmental crisis, if it continues to grow unchecked, will soon create a devastating water shortage for millions of humans, animals, plants and trees. Now more than ever, the sacred medicine that women carry in their mouth is needed worldwide. We need their songs and we need the magnetic power of their feminine ways to attract the spirit of Water back into all the sources upon the Earth.

In my heart, I am sure our sisters are responding to this call and reclaiming ownership of the waters on behalf of all life, beginning with the waters circulating in their own bodies. My wife tells me that today around eighty percent of young women suffer from some kind of physical disorder that manifests through diverse symptoms such as acne, fatigue, menstrual cramps, or depression. From the Andean perspective, the root of these female problems is easy to discern. As we see it, the Earth and women are the same; what happens to one happens to the other. Which waters were damaged first, the ones of women or the ones of the Earth? It is hard to know, but it is certain that we need to tend to the real needs of both, women and the Earth, or neither will be healed.

As a healer, when I see a woman whose body doesn't have a strong fire, I don't consider it to be a dire situation. On the other hand, if I discover in a healing session that a woman doesn't have her waters in a healthy condition, there is reason to be alarmed. If a woman's waters are neglected, illness could be brewing somewhere in her body. In a world ruled by distorted masculine fire, neglecting waters is something that happens all the time. Just take a look at the rivers and oceans used as dump stations to recognize this truth.

As I see it, and my wife agrees, the feminist revolution should not be only about society respecting women's freedom to do the same as men but also about women having the freedom to do as women do without being judged. The right to be different is as important as the right to have equal opportunities. Marilyn says women are criticized for being feminine, for the importance they give to feelings, for their natural capacity to navigate the chaotic aspect of any reality, and for their ability to multitask without needing linear order in their way of doing things. All these are feminine qualities related to the power of water that women carry in their bodies. She also explained that in her previous relationships men had tried to put her down with their rational thinking and demanded she be as rational as they were when trying to resolve a problem. Following the feminine wisdom of running water wasn't an option.

It is so crucial that women worldwide reclaim their role as owners of the Earth's waters. The song of the stars lives in the waters. Many of our current problems will only be resolved using this ageless, cosmic and primordial feminine wisdom. There is a new feminist revolution brewing in our society. This time it is led by the sacred feminine principle looking to regain its place in human life, and it is based in love and solidarity rather than fighting against men. Based on the natural laws of polarity, women will need the support and service of men allied to them. The trust between women and men needs to be rebuilt so we can be partners in the mission.

The environmental imbalance we call global warming is a globalized destructive relationship between fire and water. In essence, there is too much fire, too much heat. The waters are being disturbed, wrongly moved out of their natural containers and placed in artificial containers, then melted, contaminated, over-used and over-evaporated, creating a huge shortage of this precious giver of life in some places and a tremendous overabundance in other places as droughts and floods become more and more frequent. In addition, the history of wars is a story of the increase of fire on the planet, particularly the destructive kind of fire. Even in peacetime, the leaders of most corporations use war strategies with lots of fuel and fire in order to defeat their competitors. The winning companies, along with those who consume their products, are responsible for producing a quantity of heat that could make the Earth unsuitable for human habitation in less than a hundred years. The work of oil companies has been the most harmful in the decades leading up to the environmental catastrophe of today. The oil extracted from the depths of the Earth fueled the fires of the engines that fed the development of a modern world no longer in communication with Nature.

The corporations, typically led by exclusively masculine intelligence, did not realize that continuing to feed big fires that do not serve the health of water but instead destroy its natural containers is suicidal. How can anyone or anything continue living without healthy water? It is necessary that women take care of their waters, but it is equally necessary that men become wiser. The real wisdom of the masculine is to serve the feminine well. The gift of the masculine is to help contain and gently influence the waters of the feminine with reverence and respect and without blocking the natural flow, helping just enough for the feminine to feel the good company and support of a grounded partner.

We men learn to cultivate our masculine nature by observing the behavior of the Sun, following its movements from solstices to equinoxes. We can also learn by regularly consuming plants that carry the instructions of the Sun in them. In the Andes, women and men alike chew coca leaves, but men do it a bit more. Visitors to our homelands may mistakenly think that the ritual of chewing coca leaves is a privilege of the men when the truth is anyone can chew as many coca leaves as they want. However, men are more in need of the teachings of the Sun, so we do it more often.

The fire of the Sun has a powerful influence on the waters of the Earth, helping them to evaporate just enough to become clouds and then fall as rain, perpetuating the natural cycles of water that nourish all life. As powerful and necessary as he may be, the Sun has the wisdom to know when to soften his fire, when to retire at night and how to be gentler in the winter so the waters are at times without his direct influence and can receive the light of the Stars and the Moon. At night, the waters develop their cooler nature and follow their own rhythm and wisdom.

Snuffing out all fire is not the solution for the waters to recover from the damage done to them. As much as we cannot live without water, we equally cannot live without the Sun. We need these two opposites to work well together. In my own efforts to become a better partner of women, I always ask them to help illuminate my understanding. A good female friend of mine, whose husband is also my dear friend, recently told me something I suspected was true: women need to recognize when their words and actions extinguish their man's fire, making him either retreat or become forceful. For several years, they had some difficulties in their relationship because every time she expressed her view about something, she would insist on stating what she thought was right and he would end up becoming angry and distant. Recently she went to a lecture given by a wise woman who explained how women can unknowingly "castrate" their men and shut down their male potential instead of helping them grow. When she next visited me she said, "I know you have been trying to tell me this for years, but I was only open to hear it from another woman." She said the lecture helped her realize that she didn't really understand men and had been foolishly trying to change her man from a strictly female viewpoint, without knowing the innate tendencies of his male nature. I had been worried for them up to that point. But once she could see that her husband had to go away from her sometimes in order to preserve his fire, she was in a much better position to do her part in the work of their marriage. On the other side, her husband now has more room to grow, to learn how to be more present and stay in the climate of their sometimes conflicted relationship without running away.

When men are absent, the waters of women and children connected to them may feel uncontained, like a river with broken banks, and can move erratically, creating damage and self-destruction and then begin seeping away and eventually vanishing. Just as in Nature, destructive feminine movements are occasionally very healthy for the family as they help move stagnant energies. But constant movements of this sort that stem from a chronic lack of masculine support are not healthy. It is common for an undeveloped man to feel angered by this destructive feminine behavior and call his woman crazy, not realizing that it was his lack of presence that caused the craziness in the first place.

I am learning all of this by virtue of listening to women speak about how they see things. Some of my female friends have told me they feel attracted to men whose masculine fire is strong and well-contained, well-centered and well-managed. This shows me that we men need to recognize when we get carried away and exude too much masculine energy, burning the entire forest with our fire, drying the waters of all that is feminine, especially the bodies of our women partners. When a man's presence is always too fiery, the waters in the bodies of the women and children around him evaporate to the point of dryness and their tears and laughter do not rise easily. The masculine must take great care not to burn everything and evaporate all the waters for when the wet forest becomes a dry desert and the heat provokes more wind than water, the winds will become overly strong and destructive. In our bodies, the winds are our thoughts. The Kogi warned us that modern people need to think better thoughts or the world will be destroyed. Our fire and water need to be in good relationship so that good winds will blow through our minds — gentle, moist, creative thoughts that help us build a good reality together.

When a woman and man heal their relationship, they are healing the environment because they are bringing back the balance of fire and water on Earth. For those committed to do the healing it is useful to remember that men, as well as women with a prevalent masculine fire, have a strong tendency to be linear. This is one of our great gifts as we can stay focused and keep going in a certain direction for long periods. With this talent, we help organize our families and communities so that resources and time are used wisely to achieve many necessary goals. At the same time, there is the potential destructive aspect of this goal-oriented behavior that drives modern society because linear thinkers often keep moving forward without recognizing the impacts and by-products of their constant action. Also, a powerful linear movement toward a goal will frequently bulldoze the obstacles, as we forget to go around them by using a truly feminine resource: curves!

I do not feel we need to eliminate the masculine goal-oriented drive from human behavior. What we need is more feminine curves! When a river or any other form of energy in motion runs straight for a very long way, it becomes too fast, unstoppable, and eventually cold and destructive. Thankfully women are less linear and have beautiful curves, like the healthy rivers. The feminine mind, which is related to the Spirit of Water, knows the art of sinuous motion that is soft, slower, warm and very magnetic. The fiery masculine leaders of our society would greatly benefit from applying their love for curves to their work, reducing all sorts of collateral damages. Instead of barreling ahead like a train dead set on its destination, the feminine adapts to the contours of Nature, to what is naturally ready to happen, listening to a multiplicity of voices that compose the totality of what is true in the moment and continues moving forward even when some may think it is going sideways.

CHAPTER FIFTEEN

CHAWPIN

THE PLACE OF THE MIDDLE

Our internal fires have a strong influence on our body's waters. A good example of this is when the energy centers of the crown and the forehead, associated with the pineal and pituitary glands, are activated by practices like meditation, ceremony or lovemaking and the water in our mouth becomes powerful medicine. This formation of medicine in the mouth also occurs when the energy center of the throat produces the vibrations of sacred, tender, healing speech or singing. This is not easy to do, but it can be done. It requires years of polishing oneself and acting with deep, clean intentions. I know people who have noticed a distinct change of the taste in their mouth during lovemaking, ceremony, or another experience of union with the Sacred. They said it was like taking a sip of water from the highest, purest lake in the world and tasting a refined nectar, at once so powerful and delicate, a sensation of elevated freshness lingering in their mouth and their soul. This high quality water of their saliva was refined within the body.

In its most elevated state, the water of our mouth is like the water that springs from the land where animals can come to drink. It is the water of someone who has become a vessel of generosity. In the central Andes of Peru, we have the sacred place called Chavin where the ancient people went to learn how to be truly generous and make of themselves a refined offering for the well-being of all life. Through the practices followed there, the people of Chavin learned to illuminate the waters of their bodies and have an abundance of good medicine to give to the world.

As it was mentioned before, Chavin was originally called Chawpin, meaning "the place of the middle." The temple of Chavin is many thousands of years old and became well known because of the sculpted stone heads that were found nailed to the external walls of the building. When I first visited this sacred site and saw those heads, I realized they were all very different, each one expressing the full development of one of the individuals who lived at Chavin and made a complete journey into awakening. The temple served those dedicated individuals as an instrument for their spiritual work, an instrument that worked due to the presence and movement of water. A big square pool was built in front of the temple at Chavin for its water to collect the light of the Sun and the Stars. This water was then directed through channels from the pool into the building and circulated within the walls of dark rooms located underground. Just as we have water under our skin, water moved under the stone skin of the temple's rooms. This water, that first collects light and then circulates as powerful medicine, is *Ch'askakunaq takin*, "the singing of the stars."

There were many teachers at Chavin, and the Spirit of Water was one of the most powerful among them. The location of the temple was carefully chosen at the intersection of two rivers, the Mosna and the Wachiksa. Friends of mine who have studied Chavin have discovered that the waters circulating in the walls of the temple produced a constant sound, one whose vibrational frequency was meant to awaken the mind and spirit of those who performed their spiritual practices inside the building. These were the Andean yogis of ancient times, sages who became enlightened through receiving the frequency of the "singing of the stars" for many days without interruption while sitting in total darkness. And, because in Andean culture everything works in reciprocity, once the sacred inner powers of those sages became fully activated by their prayers and practices and through the help of sacred plants, the luminous state of their beings then radiated back toward the water circulating in the walls. As this spiritually charged water came out of the building, it irrigated the crops around the temple so they became power foods and continued running through the fields as medicine for people and life forms down the road. The water streaming out of the temple was the equivalent of a man's ejaculated semen that generates new life.

There are many signs indicating that Chavin was built as an instrument to activate the potential sacred powers of a human being so people could transform from being consumers of energy into producers of energy. In one sense, the temple was built as a mirror in which humans could see the sacred powers of their own temple, the physical and energetic body where their spirit dwells. There is a stone sculpture in an underground room of Chavin that in modern times has been named El Lanzon. It is the main *Wanka* of the temple, a standing rock that clearly depicts a fully-developed human being whose energy centers are all active and who has a large protrusion in the crown of the head, a bat in the forehead, and a mouth with jaguar fangs. This sculpture was to be observed for long periods of time as a sort of mirror for the apprentices at Chavin to activate awareness of the gifts placed in their bodies. Following what it revealed to them, they learned to use their body as a magnificent temple for the storage and distribution of nourishing energies, medicinal waters and fires that illuminated and gave vitality to all that their words, eyes and hands touched.

I was fascinated to learn from friends of mine who have spent their life studying Chavin, that they are convinced the apprentices working in the temple's sacred chambers were mostly men while the ones guiding them were mostly women. In accordance with the temple's main teaching, it makes sense that the women, kin to water, helped the men to learn. Once again in accordance with the principle of reciprocity, these men sexually nourished the women that had helped them. This gave the women an elevated energetic state and created enhanced nourishment for the children through breast milk. This ancient model of communitarian energy efficiency was built upon the laws of Nature. Mutually benefiting each other, the men and women living in the temple learned to have very energy-efficient bodies and therefore had a surplus of refined energy to give to the world.

Energy efficiency is largely missing in the modern world. Understanding it begins with knowing ourselves to the point of realizing how to take care of our internal waters and fires. Depending on our state of development, our internal waters are affected either by internal fires that originate from what the Hindus call chakras and are deeply life-giving or by internal fires simply ignited by reactions, which, like a gun in the hands of an angry child, are potentially very harmful. Unfortunately, the fires of many modern people are more reactive than life giving; moreover, people in today's world tend to exhaust their fires by constantly acting in mechanized, unconscious ways and typically under great pressure. With stress and lack of inspiration, the body becomes depleted and the inner waters lose their light, which weakens the immune system and leads to a state of poor health.

In the modern world, the sacred movement of energy within the body has become a distant abstraction. Unlike the masters of Chavin, people are needy and suffer the catastrophic consequences of being highly energy inefficient. An outer world similar to the inner world of their bodies is created by their activities, constantly depleting food and water sources and producing huge amounts of waste. Those studying to become professionals in today's world are never taught how the mismanagement of our internal waters and fires creates energetic imbalances in our bodies that promote stress and waste a good portion of our energies. How can individuals who don't know to manage their own energy manage the energy of the world? The modern world is controlled for the most part by people in a state of contraction intent on collecting and guarding personal successes. This is a widespread reality that reveals the shadow side of humanity. Like the pitch-dark rooms in Chavin's underground, humanity's shadow needs to be painted by a sacred song.

In recent times, many new young leaders have developed an awareness that didn't exist fifty years ago when the main goal was to become wealthy at all costs. Some heads of corporations and other institutions are beginning to locate the roots of our collective energy inefficiency, and they are making an effort to change the cycles of imbalance. Through the good example of these individuals, some corporations and other institutions are becoming the little Chavin for many people, the place where they are apprentices in the art of cultivating a life full of natural vitality that benefits all life. The Tibetan Lamas have a wonderful saying, "Any place is a good place to do The Work."

The management of energy is much more than an individual discipline; it is a communitarian effort. Individuals working without the solidarity of a community can rarely be truly energy efficient, regardless of how much yoga they do or how many health supplements they take. We are community-based, social creatures that do not learn or act alone. The more that the spirit of cooperation exists in a circle of co-workers or in a family unit, the more health and contentment will circulate among them and make their work, their lives and their world more energy efficient.

The ancient masters of Chavin were members of a community. They were farmers and spiritual workers connected to the sacred spirits of Nature. At Chavin, men and women deeply helped each other, humans and the forces of Nature fed one another, and all living beings engaged in a communitarian circulation of energy. Those people worked together and with the spirits of Nature to nourish a heart-centered culture where the success of one individual was always the success of everyone, of all that lives.

CHAPTER SIXTEEN

AYLLU

COMMUNITY

While we see good but forgetful people around us constantly damaging Mother Earth, we try not to do the same by dedicating ourselves to remember the old ways and do at least a little of what our ancient ancestors did. For this purpose, in front of our main communitarian house in New Mexico, there is a stone altar with a fountain of water in its center. From this sacred water, the umbilical cord that connects the Earth and the Sky grows.

In the beginning of spring when the first thunders return, we gather at this altar to bless our seeds, infusing in them the sounds of traditional sacred songs as well as the good wishes contained in our prayers. After impregnating the seeds with our heart's fire, we place them in the dark bellies of clay pots and leave them in an underground stone temple overnight to dream alive the health and happiness of the people who will be nourished by the food they will produce.

At our farm, we prepare the field for planting by making sacred designs on the ground, burying power objects, singing with drums and rattles and presenting ceremonial offerings. Our offerings feed those sacred relatives that will keep the soil watered and the farming space full of vitality: Thunders, Rivers, Winds, Mountains, Stones, Stars, the Moon and the Sun. In this way a power field is created, one suitable to welcome the seeds that carry the memory of the Universe. Just a few days after, little green creatures start popping up from the ground. The men and women of our community, who purify regularly through ceremonies of healing and communication with the Sacred, come to work in the farm early each morning, their faces still showing the effects of dreamtime, grateful for a new day and eager to offer their renewed vitality to the plants. And when some plants are ready and want to be harvested, prayers of gratitude are offered to the Sun that filled them with light and knowledge of the particular nature of our present time, and more prayers are offered to the Thunders that brought the rain and cleaned the air of our beloved land.

Cooking is a ceremony. We cook in a temple that honors the fires and waters of humanity, a simple place for the gathering of family and extended family, a place appreciated for how well it holds our human imperfection, our physical fragility, our happiness and our appetites. All the shapes, colors and sacred designs that live in the walls of the kitchen are much more than adornments; they create vibrations that activate the sacred powers of the cooks and of the food. The cooking is done with children playing nearby and tired workers sitting to converse until the time to share food finally arrives. Then we stand, holding off our hunger for just a moment longer, as a community member lifts up a spirit bowl containing bits of everything we will eat and prays aloud. The spirit bowl is a humble offering that expresses our gratitude to the sources of the food. It also carries our prayer that the power of the food be sent to all those who are hungry. At the table we celebrate life, chewing flavors and colors, our bodies remembering the voices of thunders that brought the rain that watered our nourishment and the sunlight that gave immense power to little sacred creatures like corn, potatoes, carrots, tomatoes, beets and many different kinds of greens. With innocence and joy, we feel the delicious memory of the Earth in our mouth, chest and belly and avoid talk about work as our body celebrates the arrival of its sacred instructions.

When the people of our community receive this type of nourishment, they return to the field the next day full of vitality and infuse their gratitude and strength into more plants. In this way, human talent feeds the natural cycles and everything that has the power to give life continues growing and growing. Instead of working on the farm, some of our people might create precious objects with their hands or go to our ceremonial spaces to elevate their vibrations toward the clouds, or they might even have juicy conflicts, all of which, in its way, is energy that feeds that which feeds us.

Because we have been receiving our food in this sacred manner for some time, now we are beginning to remember. And the more we remember, the more we sense something bothering us, the trembling in our insides of something not yet remembered. In the quiet moments by the fire at night, questions arise about the wisdom of our ancestors. How did they use their minds? To what extent did their well-fed bodies and spirits simply know the truth?

Our ancestors were wise without the schools we have today. They built wonders, structures sound in architectural precision that also had heart and spirit and emitted a vibration that elevated the people and the land. Their intelligence was not rooted in concepts but in storing the help they constantly received, the energy that served as fuel to cultivate specific states of being. They were keenly aware that humans are essentially two in nature, one that forgets and one that remembers, so they used ceremonies to constantly renew the states of being they intended to cultivate, never assuming any state reached was permanent. The beautiful ceremonies and powerful medicines we inherited from them give us clues about how they cultivated states of high intelligence, high awareness and great compassion. And these clues clearly demonstrate that for the most part, even when done in solitude, the cultivation of a person is part of a collective work, one that powerfully influences the health and growth of a community.

A community that follows a sacred way of life is like the tiny ring in the heart of a spiral from which bigger and bigger rings grow, extending towards the larger spheres of Universe. This can also be perceived in reverse. The big rings of the Universal Life become smaller and smaller until they form the final tiny one in the center, the place we call home where we receive our nourishment and from where we perceive the rest of the Universe.

There is a difference between being outside of something sacred and being inside of it. Communitarian life teaches us always to be inside the sacred circles of life. In the modern world, most people do not belong to a community so their tendency is to be an outsider watching Nature and the Universe from a distance, seeing them as phenomena separate from humanity, speaking about them, trying to understand them, admiring them or else wanting to figure out how to use them. Indigenous peoples and their communities are consciously inside the energy that circulates in the Earth and the Universe, communicating with these greater bodies. The ancient ones who initiated the growth of communities and tribes worldwide intended humanity to be at home within Nature, to form villages guided by Universal Instructions in all aspects and activities of their communal life.

The sacred way of life depends on good circulation of energy for its well-being, so community members must take responsibility for the energy circulating among them. Anything that blocks the circulation of energy is seen as illness. As we now build new communities in the modern world, the great challenge is to step away from the culture of winners and losers that glorifies personal success. Without changing this aspect of the modern mentality, people will resist communitarian work in which individual winners are not important. It may help to understand that, in the game of making energy circulate for the well-being of all, the moment it is only one individual who wins, the game ends and everybody loses. When this happens a huge amount of energy stays trapped in one individual and it stops circulating for the benefit of all. A healthy and sustainable human culture can never be successfully built with this type of competitive model.

There is a huge difference between a culture where parents teach their children to be perfect and a culture where parents teach their children to pray. Our indigenous ancestors were not interested in perfection or surface personal achievement. They were interested above all in honoring relationships and leading humble lives without graduations and awards, lives of permanent learning and constant renewal. For our small community in New Mexico, teaching our children to live in an indigenous way is about teaching them to pray, to sit humbly with their imperfections and always remember to ask for help. From a very young age, our children learn to offer tobacco to a plant before cutting her leaves to make medicine and are given the opportunity to sit under a tree holding a stone or a feather until they receive answers to their questions. In so doing, they develop their own relationships and alliances with the Sacred Powers that live in the other rings of the spiral around the corner from us and they learn not to depend on human intermediaries. In a simple, almost effortless way they become familiar with living inside the web of life directly influenced by its creatures and energies, some known and others mysterious. Knowing we are insiders in the realm of Nature and not outcasts of the beauty and power of the Universe is our cultural source of safety. We always feel welcomed in the wilderness of the Sacred where we continually make ourselves available to be touched, moved and cared for by something much more powerful than us.

The Sacred is simply something with high vibrational frequency that has immense power, lots of medicine, and therefore the capacity to elevate what it touches above the dense states of being that create sadness, fear, and self-centeredness. In a community, the Sacred has to be present especially in the couples that raise the families of the village. A sacred marriage is the kind of marriage that works and thrives where so many marriages today do not. A sacred marriage grows out of the couple's commitment to constantly elevate each other through respect, attention, affection and the conscious movement of their sexual energy. The high energy produced by such a couple blesses their home, attracts blessings for their family and for the surrounding community and radiates out to bless the world. In turn, the couple is supported by the powers of life that the energy of their relationship feeds, and are always given all they need to continue their journey together in the best possible way.

The marriage relationship is a powerful place to do "the work". All of us who are married know what it takes to build a good relationship, a work that is both joyful and difficult. A couple is comprised of two that are very different so they always need help. Great suffering arises when a couple does not belong to a community. Caring for children and maintaining economic health take lots of work, and time is always too short to complete all that has to be done. In a community with many aunts and uncles and brothers and sisters, everyone shares the work and the care of the little ones. This way parents can continue to develop their individual talents as well as take time to be together, precious times of rest that are not about resolving problems or planning the future but simply about sharing their waters and fires in enjoyment.

Often a couple believes the difficulties in their relationship belong to them only. The truth is usually that the problems any one couple is trying to resolve are issues held in common by others. And what is common belongs to the community. Like everything that lives, the couple needs an owner. The owner of the couple is the community, a bigger entity capable of containing, guiding and caring for the couple's needs. The experience of all community members builds the collective wisdom that helps the couple navigate their common problems and shelters their sometimes broken hearts and confused minds. Communities that sustain the couples who sustain the families that make the communities are a good example of energy efficiency. Isolation and individualism aren't energy efficient even when used to protect our energies from being drained by others. Relying on our limited individual energy can only make us impoverished, stressed and incapable. Connected to our relatives, we are wealthy and can face what seems to be impossible with great enthusiasm.

Many different groups in the world are part of a huge collective effort to return to a communitarian way of life, aspiring to cohabitate on a piece of land where they can become self-sufficient. I believe this is happening because the Earth wants it. This immense human effort reminds me of the impressive journey of the salmon. Once a year, the salmon travel thousands of miles from where they live in the middle of the ocean all the way to the mouth of the river where they were born. They travel upstream in that river against the current for many miles at grave danger. Those who survive this arduous journey arrive to the precise place where their ancestors gave life to them, ready for their final mission: to lay their eggs and give life to a new generation in the place of origin of the salmon. It seems hard to understand why they do something so difficult but, in many ways, humanity is doing the same when we seek our roots and want to return to the place where our ancestors started their wise way of life.

A few times, those who have created intentional communities have asked me for advice, particularly after they realized how easy it is to fail after only a short time. It is such a delicate situation, especially when big efforts had been made, including buying land together and people leaving their stable jobs. I have learned the only good advice I can give relates to the commitment to be humble. It is often clear to see how individuals trapped in seeking recognition and rewards for their work become more invested in the wellbeing of "me" rather than the wellbeing of "we". Belonging to a community is like being a delicious little bean in a great soup; it is better not to separate from the others in order to be special or recognized. In communitarian life we learn to become interdependent instead of independent. Anyone can ruin the community by thinking that he or she alone can make the world, and they can ruin their own lives as well, ending up alone. It is really worth it to work hard at being a really good bean instead of trying to be the whole soup!

CHAPTER SEVENTEEN

PACHAKUTI

CHANGE OF TIMES

The times are changing and enthusiastic people from all over the world are beginning to develop a new culture, one that again incorporates some of the original wisdom of ancient societies. One of the most important tasks of our generation is to collectively mend the split between the genders and between many other complementary opposites. It is crucial that we mend the division made by the sword that cut between feminine and masculine, men and women, head and heart, spirit and matter, sacred and profane, dark and light, above and below, left and right, outside and inside, earth and sky, chaos and order, and humans and Nature. The damage inflicted upon the ancient temples of the Earth People correlates to the damage made to the unity of all opposites, including the unity of men and women, the altar from which we all are born.

One of the biggest roots of all the splits we suffer from in the modern age is war between nations. Modern people trying to find their way back to their ancient origins, like the salmon swimming upriver, first have to face the cruel reality of Post-Traumatic Stress Disorder (PTSD). A huge number of people with recent ancestors that participated in wars, even several generations ago, suffer from PTSD, sometimes without even realizing it. The symptoms are inherited from one generation to another or perpetuated because those with severe trauma often provoke trauma in others. A common symptom of this disorder is a blockage in the heart, manifested as the incapacity to give and receive affection. During war, soldiers withdraw from feeling too much affection for anyone that may be killed. They also tend to freeze their affection for those they might abandon if not making it back home. Even after the war is over, the reverberations of the trauma they endured makes the former soldiers continue protecting themselves in the same way. And then their children and grandchildren often do the same even if they didn't experience the war. Likewise, warriors that had to take someone else's life will very often close to receiving tender affection afterward; the blood on their hands makes them feel no longer worthy of the gift of love. All of this creates the foundations for the development of a human culture based in trauma and personal defense. As Andean people know very well, tenderness and affectionate relationships are what a human culture really needs to stay healthy and alive. When trying to build a better human society, the healing of PTSD is not something that can be left aside.

For many generations after a war, all the implications of the traumas eventually create a whole different cultural way in which the expression of love and affection between men and women, parents and children, and all relationships are often very difficult and uncomfortable. Going to the other extreme, the relations become overly passionate, dramatic and exaggerated. It is also true that post-war societies have an extremely diminished expression of the feminine side of humanity. During times of warfare, empowering the warriors is the priority. Men and women alike will empower the warriors because they are the ones who will protect the community from annihilation. When indigenous nations were at war, all the spiritual energy of the tribe's ceremonies, even the most sacred ones, was directed toward the warriors. The tendency, in indigenous societies and in most cultures throughout the history of wars, has been to place females behind the males who protect them, and far enough away so the warriors have no sexual or emotional distractions. Everyone agreed on this, men and women alike, because everyone wanted their homes and children protected. But disempowering the feminine in order to win a war was a big price to pay. In some way, the nation's homes may not have been physically destroyed but they were severely damaged when the wonderful presence of the spontaneous feminine wisdom was lost, and its beauty and tender love were replaced by harsh or polite relationships.

The historic empowerment of men established male authorities who led the armies, and all other authorities and community councils became secondary. When the war extended for too long or when there was war after war, as was the case in many parts of the world, a social order solidified in our modern culture making all authority masculine in nature, even when that authority is held by a woman. After prolonged wartime, human power began to be seen only as masculine and males felt entitled to be served by females without necessarily serving them in return.

When this tendency, combined with the effects of PTSD, entered into sexual relationships, the possibility of true deep communication between two spirits in the intimacy of lovemaking was blocked. During and after the war, many children were born from these blocked relations that involved a union of bodies and not spirits. These children grew up struggling to find their own spirit, their own essential being. They consented to simply do what they were told and didn't follow the will of their own inner sacred power. At school and at home, they received an education that taught them to ignore their feelings in order to move safely and securely in the world, complying with what was expected from them. These children became emotionally stifled or found out that they could retaliate with highly aggressive or self-destructive behaviors, bullying others or hurting their parents by hurting themselves. They learned that feelings, dreams, spiritual guidance, or being truly affectionate or openhearted leads to a vulnerable and dangerous state that is to be avoided at all costs. The current dominant culture on Earth was built around this avoidance, for it is dangerous to be soft and inclusive in a world with so much war.

Placing men with major war trauma into roles of leadership in our society was a huge unconscious mistake. Giving too much priority to defense and security involves a big loss to the health of the culture. But this was accepted because so much pain had been inflicted on people that they didn't want to see one more child killed or another house devastated by the fires of war. Some powerful countries tried, and still try, to protect their people from war by making more war, always thinking it will be the last one that they need to win in order to dominate the world and make it safe. What an illusion! The cycle of war never ends. PTSD constantly perpetuates the internal wounds, the anger, the desire for vengeance, and the repression of the feminine for many generations.

Humanity will finally find relief from this sickness when the heart of the new culture now beginning has more fully developed. This new culture is not centered in fear but in the liberation of human talents, the feminine ones, the masculine ones and those in which the feminine and the masculine are beautifully combined. Millions of young people around the world believe in this new culture and are working hard to heal their hearts and the split of pairs within themselves. Together we are creating a new design for our society where being split is no longer the norm.

I call it a new culture, but it isn't really new. Andean people understand that we have arrived to a time called *Pachakuti*, a word that refers to a transition to a new cycle, a strong curve in the movement of time that creates big changes. The literal meaning of *Pachakuti* is "time that returns." In our culture, we have learned that everything moves in circles, so there is a point when an old time returns to infuse its character into a new time. We are now in this *Pachakuti* that brings back the light, a time of great opportunity, as when a little child receives a transmission of wisdom from a grandparent. This is a cosmic moment that carries the opportunity to retrieve ancient wisdom of humanity that was forgotten after the great split happened.

Some people feel we humans are a plague to the

Earth, inherently reckless, selfish and destructive creatures, but I know this isn't true. Before the essential work in the ancient temples was interrupted, humans were not perfect, but they lived following their heart and the heart of the Earth. For many generations, the ancient cultures of the Andes where I was born were able to balance power and compassion. In the precious times when those nations were dedicated to build peace, men and women shared a solid partnership and together wove a wise way of life. We carry the genetic memory of these ancestral times when humans inhabited a world where all creatures were respected and heard, and where no human or another life form was hungry because everyone was given what they needed. The ancient people were advanced as listeners and apprentices of forms of life who have been on Earth much longer than humans. Staying in close relationship with them, they had access to more accurate information and teachings than we do today.

In those times, the Earth People practiced a culture that brought the polarities of life into a strong unity in their hearts. The children learned to sing the songs of all the forms of life inhabiting the sacred landscape of their homeland - a practice that still continues in some aboriginal nations around the world. A boy grew up seeing older men loving and respecting the Earth and loving and respecting women in the same way. A girl saw older women love the Earth as they loved themselves, supporting each other and caring for the men who were their partners in the generation and protection of life. This expression of love was not an idea; it emerged from the whole body and spirit and was very powerful. It ended when wars and extremely hard life conditions put damaged men in charge of our homes and gave rise to machismo tendencies.

Security seems to be the priority of modern nations. For ancient cultures, the priority was circulation of energy between all types of relationships, opposites, different and equals. Seeking only to shield nations and the businesses that fuel economies from potential dangers creates a contraction of human nature, a self-protective tendency that is not productive, not even for capitalism. A culture of circulation of energy is expansive, fearless and fueled by the fire of masculine direction as much as by the unpredictable, unplanned and beautiful movements of the feminine that are akin to water.

CHAPTER EIGHTEEN

PAMPACHAY

FORGIVENESS

I remember a session I had with a group of wonderful people in Petaluma, California in which together we observed the power of consecrating all the elements of our lives. Instead of separating things as sacred or profane, I expressed how indigenous people are in the practice of consecrating all the various objects we interact with on a daily basis to keep them healthy or purify them if necessary, just by uplifting them with a prayer while incensing them.

In remote indigenous communities, when the day's water is brought into the home in the morning, it is consecrated with a prayer. By infusing it with sacred speech, the water is elevated to a high vibration and will then consecrate all that she touches and nourishes. The same is done with the natural environment surrounding the home, including all the nearby mountains, rivers, lakes, rocks and trees. We simply greet each of them in a tender and respectful manner and offer them the same coca leaves or tobacco with which we will consecrate the water in our mouths.

In Petaluma that day, we collectively realized how important it is for humanity to keep these ancient practices alive. We enjoyed a playful conversation discovering we could consecrate so many parts of our daily lives, such as the shoes we walk with, the clothes and adornments that we wear, plus our pots and pans, our beds and so much more. We all felt such joy realizing everything can be consecrated, remembering that as humans we have the capacity to pray, sing, dance, incense, and infuse everything with vibrations of high frequency to elevate them.

Then a great question arose, "If everything can be consecrated, how can we consecrate trauma?" After several different people proposed possible ways, my friend Sophie said what we were all waiting to hear, "Trauma is consecrated by forgiveness." No one could disagree with Sophie's simple answer, but it changed the energy among us as we had now entered a more difficult conversation. Yes, it is true trauma can be consecrated by forgiveness but there are complex questions to address. One woman asked, "If I consecrate the one who sexually abused me when I was little, will he be better?

Will doing this prevent others from causing harm in the same way? Will it make me feel better and less fearful?" This inquiry led us into a very deep reflection where we saw that the answer to all of these questions was ultimately, "Yes."

My Lakota father Basil Brave Heart always speaks eloquently about forgiveness, and I find he is a great example to follow. He has warmly welcomed many, many non-tribal people onto the Pine Ridge Lakota Reservation in South Dakota where he lives. Time after time, he has embraced newcomers fully and without reservation so long as their hearts are good. And he is generous in sharing his culture, wisdom and medicine with them. By sharing what is most sacred for him with the descendants of his ancestors' enemies, I have witnessed the most powerful healing occur for them as well as for him.

I was reminded of the importance of forgiveness by a very unusual experience I had at a hotel in the city of Cusco. Because there was a nice television screen on the wall of our room, my wife and I decided to enjoy a movie together. The only one available at that hour was Mel Gibson's *The Passion of Christ*. At the end of the film, a big storm erupts in the moment of the crucifixion and, amazingly the same thing happened outside in Cusco while we were watching. As the thunder rumbled in the movie, our room was shaken by thunder coming from the sky above our hotel. More than once, when lightning struck in the movie, strong lightning flashed through the window of our room! Marilyn and I kept looking at each other in amazement. What is this synchronicity trying to tell us, we wondered.

I have heard that some Christians criticize this movie for displaying the extreme brutality inflicted upon the body of Jesus. The movie avoids any romanticized image of Jesus. It presents him as a sacred warrior who endured the most painful torture and yet kept moving forward with the mission he had accepted: to give his life for the healing of others and to feed the Earth with his blood so others wouldn't have to do so. The peak of his unwavering commitment comes when Jesus, nailed to the cross and completely broken and bleeding, says, "Father, forgive them for they know not what they do." Soon after, a soldier stabs him under the ribs with a lance and copious amounts of blood and water pour out of his body. As Jesus dies, the sky breaks open, terrifying everyone and sending them running while heavy rain and lightning pound the Earth.

I too had a difficult time watching the gruesome scenes of this movie, but I appreciated seeing what was probably the true reality of the crucifixion and the torture that took place. The movie also focuses on two sacred aspects of the life of Jesus: his very close and loving relationship with his mother Mary and an honest portrayal of the way his body was destroyed. And, just as the storm in the living environment of Cusco coincided with the storm in the movie, I recognized that what happened to the body of Jesus is much like how the body of Earth is now being destroyed by forgetful humans. In fact, everything Jesus endured in the crucifixion is parallel to what our Mother Earth is presently suffering.

Some of the images of this movie reminded me of how I feel when watching documentaries with extremely shocking images of the Earth's destruction. It is painful to see the Alaskan coastline covered for miles with plastic waste and piles of once beautiful fish lying dead or the lakes and forests of the once pristine Amazon jungle now decimated with plants and soil stained by oil and littered with dead animals. We have to consecrate all this ugliness, even somehow find the beauty in it, and truly forgive those who caused it so life on Earth may continue. People that remain tied in knots fighting each other with closed hearts will not be able to call back the Spirit of Water onto a drying land.

It has become clear to me that forgiveness is intricately intertwined with the healing of the Earth's waters. Words of genuine forgiveness have the power to change the configuration of water in people's bodies and help heal generational sicknesses. Developing ourselves to the level of saying words of forgiveness as deeply authentic as those that emerged from the mouth of a holy man dying on a cross is a tremendous challenge. I do not claim to have this power, but I need to work on it if I am to help with the healing of the Earth and the waters I love so much. Authentic forgiveness can consecrate trauma and can alter the negative effects of wrong actions. It can change the state of water; it can change everything.

Another experience that taught me a great deal about forgiveness was when I met the family of a man named Carlos who spent his life fighting for social justice in a South American country. After spending more than a year in prison because of his political activism, one day he was found hanged in his prison cell. His niece, married to a friend of mine, asked me to perform a ceremony just a few days after his death. She wanted to pray for his good passage. She was afraid the hanging had been staged and that in truth he had been murdered.

The ceremony was intense and I felt deeply moved by what I learned about the way Carlos lived and died. Although I had never met him, that night I dreamt of Carlos. In the dream, he and I were at the beach and he told me that being close to the ocean was what he liked most. His niece knew this about Carlos and when I shared my dream with her, this and other details I had no way of knowing about her uncle assured her that he had come to talk to me in my sleep. The dream was mostly a profound conversation, one of such high wisdom that in the morning I wrote down all of it that I could remember.

Carlos spoke in this way: "The main occupation of a human being is to contemplate the wonders of the Universe. But instead, we spend our life digging a hole in our mind from where nothing can be seen. Living inside this hole we tend to fight each other. Because we cannot see, we live in a world that is a product of our imagination. We keep imagining it is someone else's fault that we feel locked in, afraid and angry, defensive and aggressive, gossiping like resentful prisoners." Then the beach disappeared. Carlos crossed through a doorway and I walked behind him. We entered a room where a little girl was crying. He held her in his arms and yelled, "I am not a hero!" Then he explained to the girl that he had been angry most of his life and imposed his will on others. He told her he had been in a prison long before he was incarcerated, stuck in a hole he had dug in his mind.

What followed was a precious gift. I felt what happens when we die. Suddenly a powerful spinning motion overtook me, as if I were inside a luminous giant tornado that was moving upwards at a very high speed, so fast the words dizzy or disoriented cannot begin to describe the sensation. When the movement suddenly stopped, there was the most profound silence emanating from a strong, yet comforting, grayish white light. Carlos and I were together in the light, peaceful and content beyond all bounds until two men appeared in the scene, one with a gun and the other with a long menacing stick. I was abruptly taken to a very dark and dirty room where Carlos was screaming as the two men hit him over and over again without mercy. Then I was suddenly back in the light, watching Carlos shake hands with the two men that now looked radiant. I immediately woke up and laid in my bed astonished by all I had experienced in the dream. I immediately understood that Carlos had forgiven the men who tortured him in prison. Incredibly, I fell right back asleep and dreamt of Carlos again.

Now he was looking at the night sky from the beach, and the planets and stars were so close that we could clearly see their distinct shapes and colors and the light radiating from them. This was truly one of the most beautiful images I have ever seen in dreamtime. Before he disappeared and left me alone on the beach, Carlos said, "Peace is the only real justice available to a human being."

I am convinced that Carlos realized the men who tortured him with the utmost cruelty in prison for a year were once hurt in some similar way. When I visited with him in the spirit world through the dream, I saw his feelings of real forgiveness and even immense love towards the men. And he found peace. His niece was eager to know who to blame for his death and asked me if my dream revealed details about it. I told her that what I dreamt was what Carlos wanted her to know, that he had forgiven those men who had tortured him and didn't want them to be punished for being mentally and emotionally ill. I left her with what I thought was the most important instruction I received in my dream: "Don't wait until you are dead to come out of the darkness of your mind's hole. The Universe is so beautiful, so full of wonders, and you can see them while you are still on Earth. Seeing them should be your main occupation."

Since that dream, there are moments every day when I remember to observe and enjoy the wonders that appear in front of me. Climbing out of the mind's dark hole to see the beauty around me helps me feel better. Feeling better helps me to forgive others as well as myself, and forgiving helps me stay out of the hole. Sometimes I need only look at a cloud in the sky or a new expression of my little daughter or at any of the magical ways the spirits of Nature move before me when I take time to be still and deeply observe these gifts I receive.

CHAPTER NINETEEN

ASHKHA UNU!

ABUNDANT WATER!

From a young age, I was dedicated to helping individuals who suffered from various illnesses or from pain in their heart and confusion in their mind. At some point during my early thirties, I was called to do ceremonial work and focus more on groups. My Elders, both Andean and Lakota, gave me permission to do this service for people and for the Earth. This was a position of privilege for me because, while leading ceremonies, I had to place myself directly between the Earth and the Sky. I had to be very clear about all the directions surrounding me and also about the medicines that flow from each of them. I had to see things from a very broad perspective in order to do my work. Now, I am aware that what I was truly seeing was the wholeness of Pachamama. I could really see her and feel her in every ceremony, and it became clear that she had been damaged. Observing this over and over again, my heart hurt, and I became more committed than ever to serve her unconditionally.

My relationship with the spirit of the Earth became closer and closer and it reached a peak with a dream I had of her. In the dream, the Earth presented herself in the shape of a very rugged old woman who lived in a tiny underground house. When I approached the front door of her house, she threatened me with a big knife and threw a bunch of metallic garbage at my feet, as if to say, "When are you going to take care of this?" After expressing her anger, she quickly softened up and invited me into her house. Suddenly I found myself in a nightclub for women only. Shy and surprised, I walked in and was immediately facing the woman in charge who was the bartender and guardian of this space exclusively for women. Somehow she knew that the "old woman" had made an exception and accepted my presence there. She and the other women playfully enjoyed having me around, and I had a really good time too, flirting and laughing with them. In the last part of the dream, I was suspended a few inches above ground and flying on something similar to a magic carpet in the direction of the stone temple at our ceremonial center in New Mexico.

A couple of years later, the stone temple became the

home of the *Orco Waranka* sacred fireplace, an altar dedicated to the mission of making ceremonies at many locations worldwide for the healing and full recovery of the Earth. The heart of this altar and the blessing of carrying it in alliance with the *Apukuna*, the spirits of the mountains, came to me from my Q'ero Elder Martin Paucar of Q'erototorani in the mountains of Cusco. One very special day, my friends Miguel Angel, Alonso, Bacilio, Cindy and I sat on the ground with Tayta Martin high up in the mountains surrounded by the men, women and children of his community. As we ate potatoes together, he said that the mission my friends and I were accepting was the work of *Wiracocha*, the Sacred Source of Vitality. He shared with us how when he was nine years old, his grandfather had told him that the work for the healing of the Earth would someday happen and that some young people would come to ask for his blessing and help. That moment was the only time I have ever seen tears in his eyes.

The work of *Orco Waranka* aspired to create a network of people throughout the planet who were committed to lighting a fire on each solstice and equinox — a total of four times a year — and making an offering to the spirits of the mountains and the lakes of their local region. My work was to travel everywhere I found someone willing and capable of making this commitment and show them how to prepare the offering, then do the first ceremony with them along with their community. I had to be certain the commitment of everyone was solid so the fires would all be lit at exactly at the same hour those four times a year.

A few women had visions that helped me get oriented in this work. It all began when my good friend Ginny had a sacred dream in which she saw the Earth from outer space with little red spots all over it. She realized those spots were sacred fires all lit simultaneously for the healing of the Earth, and I understood this vision contained the instructions for a mission I was willing to accept. Soon after the Apukuna gave us their blessing through the voice of Martin Paucar, we began lighting the sacred fires. Another sister, Yaci from Uruguay, came down from a Vision Quest on the mountain with a message for me. She said, "I was visited by tall people who were made of pure white light. They said they were the *Apukuna*, spirits who live on the mountain peaks and were guardians of life on Earth who worked to keep things healthy and in balance. They asked me to tell you to keep doing the work you are doing, because it is helping them to do their work."

Imagine how happy I was to hear Yaci say this! I was encouraged and more motivated than ever. I felt the *Apukuna* spirits had given me full permission to take this prayer to all the mountains in the world. I also felt a huge sense of responsibility and so, for eight years, with the support of wonderful people I never stopped bringing this altar to new places. I was often away from home and from my little daughters for long periods of time and seemed to always be leaving soon after I had just returned. At some point this work became heavy on my body, with so many flights and a constant change of diet. It became heavy on my heart as well. The more of the world I saw, the more pain I felt, witnessing first-hand the widespread devastation of Nature and the rapid spread of a commercialized high-tech culture powered by media that had everyone overly busy, hyper-excited, highly distracted, and utterly forgetful of our Mother. On the other hand, I also had the opportunity to visit the most beautiful places on Earth and work with wonderful people, individuals from many different countries and cultures all united by the same heart who really cared for the well-being of life and were willing to do something about it. This brought me immense joy in the celebration of our shared identity as children of the Earth.

Although physically spread throughout the planet, all the communities who held sacred fireplaces did the last ceremony together connected by the *Seq'es,* the lines of energy we had built over the years, just as a spider builds her web. On December 21, 2012, thousands of us spent the day and night around our sacred fires praying for the healing of the Earth and making our generous offerings to nourish the spirits of the mountains, oceans, rivers and lakes one final time. We all sent a clear and powerful message to the Universe:

"WE WANT TO CONTINUE LIVING! AND WE WANT ALL OTHER FORMS OF LIFE WHO SHARE THIS HOME WITH US TO CONTINUE LIVING!!!"

As I sat in the underground temple that day with a wonderful group of community members all circled around the fire and around the colorful offering abundant with flowers, animal fat, coca leaves, tobacco, grains, fruits, medicinal herbs, honey, seeds, chocolate, animal cookies and sprinkles, I felt content and grateful to arrive at this moment after so many years of work. And I very much wanted to know, like someone with an open wound wants to know what medicine will heal them, if all the effort had borne any fruit, if we had been able to love our Mother enough for her to recover from her wounds and injuries.

After chewing some coca leaves and smoking some Mapacho tobacco with the others, I picked up my Shipibo rattle and began to shake it. All the achira seeds inside started singing and helped me to sing and call the rain and call for help from all the most remote places of the Universe to come into the heart of the Earth. Something sacred made me close my eyes and sing and sing for a very long time without pausing. As I sang, I saw the world being activated, first in Africa, where elephants and lions turned their heads to see where the song was coming from. I saw the elders there, the descendants of the ancient lineages of magicians, lighting sacred fires too, joining this prayer for the continuity of life, for the healing of all the pain endured by humans and Nature in modern times, praying for the return to an earthly paradise where every form of life is connected by tender and respectful relationships.

From Africa I was moved to Australia, where the Aborigines were celebrating a day they had dreamt of long ago. They invited me to dream with them for a renewed life, a life akin to the dance of the constellations in the sky. Lights vibrating in the mirrored drops of water running in the rivers were a song that nourished the trees and plants and then flowed into the mouths of the people who sang the dream of the Earth clean and clear, giving birth to millions of shiny little ones whose cries and laughter watered the crops of the renewed land.

I was then moved to Europe and saw all its ancient Earth People waking up from a long rest in the darkness, renewed by a love that spoke in foreign yet familiar languages. In Ireland, the green light and the water danced together to create a powerful healing drink that searched for mouths and cried for the return of the snakes. I saw exhausted warriors whose long white beards were wet with the tears of their women holding them beside tree trunks soft with moss. As rain fell gently, dwarf people emerged from underground after centuries, awakened by the long-awaited song of the thunders announcing a new beginning.

Time melted into sacred time and I don't know how long I was singing. I was moved through the American continent, from the South to the North, until I felt my body again sitting on the ground in our temple in New Mexico. I opened my eyes and saw sitting across from me the beautiful woman, not yet my wife, who was my partner in leading the ceremony. There was an offering arranged on top of a big manta at her feet and the fire was between us, waiting to receive all this nourishment now charged with our songs and infused with all the intentions and prayers of the people there. These were people who intensely wanted to continue living, people who believed in happiness not bound by a fear of scarcity, people with no need for approval from a society that separates Spirit and Nature, people who came often to ceremonies because they refused to become ill from lack of communication with the powers of the Universe.

Although my eyes were now open, my vision journey was not complete. Now I was seeing luminous people in our stone temple that came from far away to participate and help in the ceremony. There were at least ten of them, wearing white tunics and white pointed hats and carrying bags full of coca leaves. Three of them came near to me while the others stayed in the circle with the rest of the people. One of the three stood behind me and the other two stood on either side of me. Before us was the ancient altar with fresh glowing coals where the offering would be placed. The one behind me put his hand on top of my head and immediately I was transported into outer space where I saw lots of very bright lights shoot out of the Earth, one after the other. And I heard the beings surrounding me say, "The Earth is a Mother of Stars. All that comes down to her eventually goes up again and lands somewhere else. The light of the Stars comes down into the Earth and impregnates her. When a long cycle finishes, as it does today, the light of new Stars is born. What you are seeing is happening right at this moment. These lights are all the guides of humanity, the bright beings whose teachings and compassion guided humanity through the time that ends today. They depart to become the new Stars that will make the Universe continue growing. As the Universe grows, the Earth grows too. Today begins a new time. Most of the new guides of humanity are here, but they are babies so humanity will continue to be lost for a while longer."

They went on to say, "It is time to celebrate! Once more, the Earth has succeeded in its function as a middle place that receives what descends from the Universe and then produces what ascends to the Universe. The ascended energies that nourish the continuity of life in the Universe were created in two different ways. One was by spiritual workers using vibrations to elevate the frequency of dense life forms on Earth. The other was by common people engaging in the joys and conflicts natural to the innocent immaturity of human beings. Yes, it is true that even conflict produces energy, and the Universe doesn't waste anything produced on Earth."

To my great surprise, they then showed me wars, atrocities, and all kinds of human conflicts and told me these painful events also contributed to the production of energy the Earth used for the conception and gestation of Stars. Even what we consider to be negative is essentially energy. The Earth is so advanced in her capacity to digest and transmute toxic energies that, in the end, she makes it all into light. I understood this from the Andean perspective in which there is no good and evil, there are only light and heavy energies. When we do healing and remove toxic heavy energies that are harmful to the body, we send them down to the Earth, knowing that for her these energies are like what chocolate is for us.

It was a huge revelation to discover that all the wars of history, all the crimes of the worst dictators, the breaking of the temples of my ancestors, and so many other forms of suffering caused by actions I consider unacceptable have been transformed into light and now shine as stars in the sky of another world out in the Universe. My Andean ancestors surely knew about this powerful capacity of the Earth because when terrible things happened, they never took the stance of victims. Even in the midst of the most difficult conditions of life imaginable, they never lost their ability to find peace and happiness.

My eyes remained open and the people of flesh and bone as well as the ones that only I could see appeared equally solid and real to me. The voices of the people in white continued sounding inside me in a way I could clearly understand: "There will still be war and suffering for a while. Things will not change very fast but they will certainly change because, on this day, the man-made structures of power have been fatally injured. When the light born in the Earth's core was shot into outer space, the foundation that held these structures in place was destroyed and they will eventually crumble to nothing. We advise everyone to stop investing in a way of life that is ending. Even the world's economic system will be different at some point."

The best thing I heard, music to my ears and joy for my heart, were their final words: "We are grateful to your family all over the world and to all the families and groups that prayed in various ways and believed in the recovery of the Earth. The reward for all of you and for your communities is that you will not run out of water. The original purity and abundance of water will return to your communities to give you life."

We are at the very end of a life cycle that has lasted thousands of years. Our dear Mother Earth has completed her mission to shoot precious light out into the Universe and now she has to recover. Today she is like a woman who endured the most difficult birth and suffered a rupture that almost killed her. She requires our assistance. As far as the healing of her waters, there is some science and some spirituality to it, and we have to work with both. Opening our minds, hearts and spirits we can bring back and include original forms of communication and ways of working with Nature that are feminine like running water and very different from the high tech-based ways of the modern world.

CHAPTER TWENTY

K'ANCHAQ UNU

THE LIGHT IN THE WATER

During the time my wife Marilyn was trying to help me uncover some of the mysteries of water, one night, before falling asleep, she asked for a dream and her request was generously answered. In her dream, she saw a transparent jar full of clean water on top of a table. Inside the jar there were tiny fish swimming. Beside the table, on the ground, there was a small pond full of very murky water that Marilyn knew was very, very deep and totally dark. Then she realized she was holding a fishing line made out of shiny silver in her hand. When she dangled the fishing line into the murky waters of the pond, a very unusual looking white fish rose from the depths and jumped upward into the jar of clean water on the table.

Some older women were behind Marilyn talking to

her, helping her understand what she was witnessing. She became aware that the magic white fish with the unusual face was a spirit, the most elusive and difficult for anyone to ever see, the Spirit of Water. Marilyn was mesmerized watching the light that radiated from the magic fish. The older women told her the silver fishing line was so precious that it had to be kept safe at all times and that she should put it in some lockers that were sitting behind the table.

I spent an entire year trying to make sense of Marilyn's dream without any success. I couldn't clearly interpret why the Spirit of Water showed up as a white fish or what the silver fishing line was. But I never disregarded her dream, and I never forgot it. In the depths of my heart, that sequence of images felt like an ancient memory, like the feeling of knowing you know something but not quite remembering it, like the forgotten name of a person that is on the tip of your tongue.

Then one night I had my own dream. Actually it was a series of dreams, all with a common theme. In each of the dreams I was participating in a social event and having a good time when, at some point, an older but very vibrant woman appeared out of the blue and kissed me on the mouth. The last of these dreams was so strong that it awakened me in a state of fright. In it, I found myself in a place I can't fully describe. It was the light, the spirit world, the emptiness, or some realm different from the material Earth. A gigantic female spirit made entirely of white light, wearing a white hat and white dress, with a luminous white face without nose, eyes, ears or mouth was facing me. She was so big and so full of light that I felt small, awe-struck, and sincerely respectful of her greatness as well as fearful for my fragile life in her presence. She said to me, "Unless you want me to take you, find me someone else that I can take instead of you."

I woke up in the middle of the night trembling, feeling my family near me and thinking of the suffering they would go through if it were my time to be taken to the other world. I lived each of the next few days as if it were my last. Even when I remembered that some years ago Tayta Martin told me it is a blessing to dream that a woman who is a complete stranger kisses you because that woman is Pachamama herself, I couldn't escape the apparent message that I had to choose someone to die or that I myself would die.

One way or another, my dream definitely meant something very serious. I went to consult with a woman who has a true gift for talking to the Spirit of the Earth. She laughed when I told her it was possible I would die soon unless I chose someone to die in my place, which I would never do. Using her gifts, she discovered and then told me that before my dream I had made contact with a great water spirit at a lake. The woman I saw in my dream was a Princess of Nature, the spirit of a lake. She wanted to know if I was going to marry her or not, and she wasn't willing to wait much longer so, if I wasn't ready, I needed to find a replacement. The oracle woman also said that accepting what the spirit was offering implied letting the old arrogant male side of me die.

What she said made complete sense, and I was grateful for her capacity to *see*. A few days before my dream, I had visited a lake at a very high altitude in one of the most beautiful places I had ever been. When I kneeled and touched the lake's water with my fingers, it suddenly began hailing strongly. I knew this meant I was destined to find this lake and it would be a strong ally in my life and work. This was a day I had long awaited, and I felt so elated and grateful. Those who accompanied me there wanted to run for shelter, but I asked them not to leave in such a glorious moment and they agreed. So we opened two bottles of *chicha*, a traditional Andean beverage made out of corn. After offering the contents of one bottle to the lake, we enjoyed iced *chicha* as falling hail bounced into our glasses from the sky!

Amazingly, the oracle woman, to whom I told nothing about my visit to the lake, said to me, "A seed, like a little round ball of white light, was given to you when you were at the lake." She continued, "The information was placed in your belly and is already working on you. You have to go back there. You need to give your old masculine self to the lake and then wait for what she decides to give you in return. Be ready, she will give you much!"

I went back to the lake as soon as I could and everything took place just as the oracle woman said it would. After I gave that old and heavy part of me to the water, she gave me so much! I was blessed, purified, loved and nourished by her just like my mother did for me when I was in her womb. The gifts she gave me I must keep to myself and cannot speak about. But there was one gift I really wanted that she didn't give me. I wanted instructions about how to do healing work for the waters of the Earth. I wanted to join those making efforts to repair the severe damage to the waters and be useful in helping to prevent the thirst that is coming to all life on Earth unless things change. She told me giving instructions wasn't her way of doing things. "What I do to you has the power to change you, heal you, make you cry or make you laugh, but I am not the one that gives direction in the way you are asking." So she sent me to another lake to receive the instructions, a male lake that I had heard was the place where Inca Pachakuteq himself received his instructions a very long time ago.

My friend Miguel Angel and I traveled to this lake together. He had been there before and knew his way around. We took a walk around it first, very aware that we were walking exactly where our ancient grandfather Pachakuteq had walked. We felt like children given the gift of visiting the home of their hero, the enlightened Inca that guided the building of many temples that have kept the ancient memory alive for our benefit. We found a good spot to sit and had a beautiful ceremony surrounded by eagles soaring, alpacas grazing, and funny black piglets digging in the mud for something to eat. We were filled with gratitude for being so welcomed in a place of power, one that can be dangerous if one is not well received.

Many hours went by, and despite the beauty and intensity of our time singing and praying, I didn't feel I had received my instructions. Then suddenly, sitting by the lake, my mind went totally still and my eyes focused on the light reflected in the very little waves in the water. There were lots of forms, like white fish made of light, appearing and disappearing together like an undulating, intermittent luminescence dancing over the water. Each one of them looked like the magic fish from my wife's dream! I gazed at them with my mind empty for a brief moment that felt like a very long time, and then clearly felt something enter my body and jolt me with a surge of power. It was as if I had eaten what I had seen, the light touching the water. I remained very still for quite a while afterward, waiting for the lake to give me my instructions before we left. The only response was a feeling of certainty in me that I had already received them through my eyes and my breath. As always happens, one day I would feel inspired, reach a state called *Yuyay*, remember, and be truly intelligent once again.

I will remember how our inner waters keep our spirit attached to our body and keep us alive in the same way that lakes, rivers and oceans have the power to keep the spirit of the stars attached to the Earth. I will make use of this memory when the time arrives for me to participate in the making of lakes, waterfalls and springs. I will remember to look at what is above as much as what is below. The water of my word will ask for help from the Sacred Powers. The light touching the water in my eyes will show me where to dig. The voice of my ancestors vibrating in my blood will tell me how a human becomes Nature doing the work of Nature, like the Inca that built lakes in the highest places of the Andes, or the Buddhists that built the ancient reservoirs of Sri Lanka where life thrives even amidst excruciating heat. Just like those Inca and Buddhists did long ago, I must be hearing an irresistible call from the beloved Spirit of Water for there is nothing I want more now than to build new homes for her abundant presence.

EPILOGUE

When we work for our beloved Mother Earth with the desire to support her wellness, it isn't enough to count on good concepts and ideas. In order to have a real influence on the state of the Earth, we need to perform actions that have power. And not all actions have power. Even with great concepts, advanced technology and lots of money, we still may perform actions with no significant influence on the Earth or that may even interfere with what would naturally unfold. Our actions have power when they rise directly from what has accumulated within us through years of receiving nourishment from the Sun, the Earth and the Stars. After consuming sacred waters and power foods charged with instructions, after learning to listen to our allies in the natural and spirit worlds, we know what to do and how to do it. The power of our actions is then rooted in the state of our being, in the fierce commitment of our heart, in how available we are to be moved by something sacred, and in the frequency of our vibration and the energy stored in our body to fuel our actions.

Concepts are simply reminders. They keep our attention on something important we don't want to forget, an understanding that gives clarity to our mind and directs our actions. But a concept is not powerful by itself. The concept of freedom, for example, reminds us of a precious state of being we don't want to lose but the concept alone has no power to make someone free.

Our mind is strong when it is connected to Nature. A healthy mind is like a boomerang we throw out into Nature, into the wilderness of the Universe, and catch when it returns to us with everything it has recorded on its journey. A healthy mind needs to circulate in open spaces, like any other energy, otherwise it gets stuck conversing with itself. And all energies that are stuck become unhealthy. In cities, people typically don't live in daily contact with the wilderness, so it becomes easy to have a mind that follows only ideas and not the guidance of Nature. People that grow up in cities are at greater risk to believe that concepts have power in and of themselves. A mind that is always immersed in an urban environment and fed mainly human-made information can become an impoverished mind, one deprived of that which moves in the vastness of the wilderness or the deep waters of the sacred feminine sources of life.

There will be a revolution in the modern human mind once it is truly freed and allowed to travel far outward, remembering once again that Nature and the Cosmos contain much more accurate information than any human database. Our minds need to breathe in very broad spaces and receive energy from Universal Sources more than human ones. The efforts of marketing can also be a limitation to those working for the well-being of the Earth because marketing involves taking energy only from other humans in the form of money and other support. Marketing is the art of convincing other humans to give you their energy. By contrast, ceremony is the art of inviting the Sacred Powers of the Universe to give you their energy. The energy of humans is always limited, and even those with abundance and genuine generosity could eventually become contracted and protective and afraid to lose what they have. The Universe is an endless and fearless source of vitality, like an infinite well.

In response to our sincere requests, the sacred energy in motion of the Universe gives us nourishment to increase our internal power and the power of our actions. It gives us instructions that guide and organize our actions, and creates the right "weather," the right conditions to support the success of our actions when they truly serve the well-being of all life or their failure when we have something important to learn.

ACKNOWLEDGEMENTS

I give thanks to all those with whom I had the conversations that inspired me to write this book. It was my friend David Tucker from the Pachamama Alliance who first told me this book was needed. Thanks to his suggestion, I embarked on a journey that brought many memories and much ancient wisdom back to my heart. My wife, Marilyn, continually helped me see the feminine side of things. Without her energy and input, this book would never have been conceived.

Thank you, *Ate*, Basil Brave Heart for your wisdom and for carrying the teachings of your Lakota ancestors. Thank you, my dear friends in Cusco: Miguel Angel Pimentel, Bacilio Zea Sanchez, Rene Franco, Vicente Quispe, Silvia Maza and Maria for sharing what you know about our Andean Culture. And very special thanks to a Peruvian sage, Mario Osorio Olazabal, who allowed me to sit and hear him make observations about the observations of our ancestors. My discussions with him shined much light in my mind, especially in relation to how the people of places like Chavin and Machu

Picchu built their sacred reality.

In creating this manuscript, I consulted with other authors, my friends Claude Poncelet, Jochen Zeitz and Timothy P. McLaughlin whose input and recommendations contributed to the clarity and depth of this work. I am very grateful to them. Towards the end of the editing process, led by Timothy P. McLaughlin, I also received valuable help from Cynthia Tunga Frisch, for which I am very grateful. And I also want to give thanks to Mark Mooney, Madeline Wade and Sophie Cooper for their good advice and artistic contributions.

My eternal gratitude goes to my dear Q'ero elder Martin Paucar, who made his journey back to the stars while I was writing this work. Tayta Martin was a man who spoke to Pachamama like someone deeply in love talks to his beloved, a man who really knew how to love everything and everyone without ever judging. I dedicate this work to him as well as to my dear sister Jeannie Kerrigan and my dear uncle Bill Brave Heart. Good journeys to the three of you. You live on in my life.

Urpillay Sonqoyay wayq'eykuna, panaykuna.
Urpillay Sonqoyay Apukuna.
Urpillay Sonqoyay Illa Teqsi Wiraqocha.
Kausachun Pachamamachay!

My little heart a little dove (thank you) brothers and sister.
My little heart a little dove (thank you)
Great Spirits of the Mountains.
My little heart a little dove (thank you)
Abundant Source of Vitality, Foundation of the Light.
Live, my little Mother Earth!

GLOSSARY

Altomisayuq: The highest development of a Spiritual Leader touched by lightning.

Allin: Good.

Allyu: Community, Extended Family.

Amaru: Sacred Snake.

Apukuna: Spirits of the Mountains.

Ashkha: a large quantity.

Cannunpa (Lakota): Sacred Pipe of the Lakota. Pronounced *chanupa*.

Chaska: Star.

Chawpin: The place of the middle.

Chicha: an Andean traditional beverage made out of corn, also known as *Ajha* in Runasimi.

Ch'uspa: Andean bag.

Cincasa (Lakota): Smoking herb. Pronounced *chinchasha*.

Haywarikuy: To hand something with tenderness.

Heyoka (Lakota): The contrary or sacred clown.

Kay: Here, this.

K'anchaq: from the word K'ancha, a bright light.

Machu: Old man.

Mamo (Kogi): Spiritual Leader, Healer.

Mana: No, not.

Mañakuy: Prayer.

Mapacho: Tobacco from the Amazon areas in Peru.

Masintin: The complement of two that are similar.

Mikhuna: Food.

Misa: Altar.

Misayuq: The one who has the altar.

Mosqokushan: Dreaming.

Munay: To want, the will of the heart, love in action.

Munani: I want (noqa munani).

Nina: Fire.

Ñauparunakuna: Ancestors.

Orco: Mountain.

Pacha: Time, space, time-space.

Pachakuti: Change of times, the return of a time.

Pachamama: Mother Time-Space, Mother Earth.

Paha Sapa (Lakota): Black Hills.

Pakarina: The source where life is born.

Pampachay: Forgiveness.

Pampamisayuq: The one who has the altar of the territory.

Paq'o: Healer.

Pukllay: To play, carnival.

Pututo: Andean trumpet made out of a conch shell.

Phaqcha: Waterfall.

Phaqchayug: The one that has the waterfall.

Qhawana: Observatory. Comes from *Qhaway* - to observe.

Qhawashan: Observing.

Qocha: Lake.

Qorakuna: Plants.

Runa: People.

Runasimi: The Language of the Human People.

Seq'es: Energy lines that connect different spots on the land.

Shipibo: Tribe of the Amazon Area in Peru.

Supay: Someone exceptional at some discipline or type of work.

Tayta: Father, Elder.

Taki: Song, music.

Tika: Flower.

Tusuy: Dance.

Unu: Water.

Wak'a: Sacred Site.

Wanka: Sacred Standing Rock.

Waranka: One thousand.

Wilka: Sacred, Powerful.

Wira: Fat.

Wiraqocha: Divine Source of Vitality.

Yaku: Water.

Yanantin: The complement of two that are different.

Yuyay: To remember, to be intelligent. Intelligence.

Yuyaykuy: Hey, remember (with tenderness).

SOURCES

For Ancient Andean Culture:

EL LEGADO DE LA SOCIEDAD ANDINA ANCESTRAL
By Mario Osorio Olazabal

CIENCIAS ANDINAS APLICADAS
By Mario Osorio Olazabal

THE INCAS
By Franklin Pease

For Lakota History:

THE DAY THE WORLD ENDED AT LITTLE BIG HORN
By Joseph Marshall III

THE SPIRITUAL JOURNEY OF A BRAVE HEART
By Basil Brave Heart

For Kogi Wisdom:

ALUNA
Documentary Film Directed by Alan Ereira